Bedsores and Butterflies

Barbie Smith

Dearest :

Wow — I am so thankful for your love and light in my life! You make my soul smile and give me such hope for the future.

You are my love & my daughter always!

I love you! Barbie

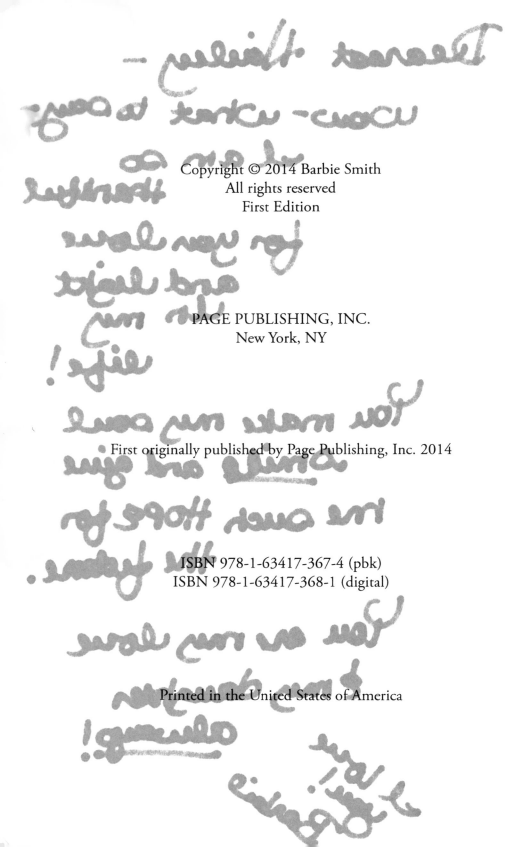

PAGE PUBLISHING, INC.
New York, NY

First originally published by Page Publishing, Inc. 2014

ISBN 978-1-63417-367-4 (pbk)
ISBN 978-1-63417-368-1 (digital)

Printed in the United States of America

Believing that all things work together for our good can be a very difficult task, especially in the face of adversity or tragedy. Keeping a positive outlook is easy on the mountaintop, but how do we fair as we pass
through the valleys of our lives?

I share the following stories in hopes that you, the reader, may
glimpse the *hope* and *peace* that I saw displayed in people's lives over
and over, in the darkest of valleys.

Death changed my life at an early age. What seemed to be the end
of me, proved to be just the beginning. I was stuck in grief for so long
that I had "bedsores" from being in one place too long. I had to let go
of some things, and hold onto some things.

All of our lives are new endings, and new beginnings. Pain, that
we may know Peace. Sorrow, that we may know Joy. Death, that we
may know Life. The Happy and the Sad, may we embrace them all,
praising *him* for the opportunity to do so.

Bedsores and Butterflies.

Chapter 1

As I stared down into the casket, my eyes hungrily tried to memorize every detail. The dark hair, the way it was combed to the side, the strong eyebrows, and the curve of his mouth. I laid my hand atop his, and my mind went back to the last time that I had touched that hand, almost fifteen years before. I was seven years old, and my sister had whisked me away for a moment during a family vacation. We were back where we were born, California. I found myself standing in a state hospital with various smells and noises I had never heard before. We stood in a large room, looking anxiously down a brightly lit hallway. My eyes strained to see him.

Suddenly, he was there and that hallway seemed to shrink with the image of the boy in the wheelchair being pushed down it. My eyes widened in fear for a moment at the sight before me. This boy was strapped in full, even his head, as constant seizures shook his eight-year-old frame. He had tumors everywhere. His head lolled to the side, and his eyes had a glassy, faraway look. He was unable to speak as the tumors were also *inside*, on his brain, and other organs.

I tried to remember him. I had been told stories of when we were toddlers, how he would come up behind me and snatch my hair out, then hold it up into the sunlight to watch it shine. He could walk and talk before this horrid disease stole those things from him and our family.

I looked at the boy beside me and fought down my fear at the sight of him. I reached out and held his hand. I began to talk to him, whispering that I loved him. Right then, he squeezed my hand! I was so excited, even as the nurses assured me it was only a reflex. I had just moments with him in that hallway, and now I stood before his casket.

I never really looked like my mom or sister, and as I stared at my brother, I longed to see similarities. I found them in his olive skin and dark hair. I held that hand that I had held so many years before. I knew this time I wouldn't feel that "squeeze" back, but I felt it in my heart "I love you too."

As a child, when I would pray or be upset, I would talk to my brother "Bobby" and pretend that we lived in a world where he was free of disease and disability, and I could have a playmate. Bobby has long since crossed over, his wheelchair and his casket is now a distant memory. He is free of that body and mind that was ravaged on this earth as he walks in perfect health and peace in heaven.

When I think of him, and the reunion we shall have one day, I can still feel the squeeze of his hand on that summer day in California, and the squeeze in my heart that I felt in that dimly lit funeral home. One day, we shall walk and talk together for all of eternity. Brother and sister, together again.

I can't wait to pull his hair.

Chapter 2

The date was April 17, 2012. The event—a beautiful, seventeen-year-old young woman leaving her car, and taking the *hand of Christ*. For all of us "left behind," it was a horrible tragedy the day that Kambrin Sophie Grace Dennis was killed in that car wreck.

Her light and her laugh changed any and all within the sight and sound of it.

One of the *many* beautiful things about KamBam, (so named by her momma because of how she connected with a softball), was that she was and *is* a Lady Mustang. She loved softball, and played barefoot, any chance that she got. She will forever be a lot of people's "Barefoot Angel."

Kambrin met Christ on Tuesday, and on Thursday, a broken-hearted team of Okay Mustang boys were playing in baseball districts. Despite their broken hearts, they resolved to play for Kambrin, and they won.

Kam's funeral was on the following Monday, and on Thursday, the boys now had to play in baseball regionals in Cameron, Oklahoma.

No, the name wasn't spelled the same as "Kambrin," but it sounded the *same* when you said it. Coincidence? I don't believe in it.

At one point, the boys played the team from "Cameron." As each Okay Mustang stepped up to the plate to bat, they drew Kam's number in the dirt as their name was announced. It was heartbreakingly beautiful.

And as each player from the opposing team stepped up to bat, the announcer said, "Now batting for Cameron . . . !"

Every player on that field, knowingly and unknowingly, was batting for the Barefoot Angel watching over those broken boys. I went over and shared the story with one of the moms from Cameron, who then, through her tears, insisted I tell it again as she retrieved the principal of the school.

There are those moments . . . when heaven invades earth and his kingdom comes in our hearts and souls—this was one of them for me.

Our Barefoot Angel danced above those boys, playing in the sunlight, cheering them on, loving their tenacity and strength, shouting "Let's play ball!"

And—for that moment—*son*light broke through the clouds of grief and pain. It will always prevail—we just have to be open to seeing it.

Dance on Barefoot Angel!

Chapter 3

I heard the sickening crunch of metal behind me. I had just pulled into the vacuums at a car wash I randomly went to.

As I turned toward the sound, I saw a woman's face; her jaw dropped in horror.

I jumped out of my car, and the first thing that I saw was the smoking SUV crashed into the car wash sign. Directly behind the passenger side lay the crumpled form of a man.

There were a handful of people gathered as I ran toward him. As I closed the distance between us, I kept waiting for someone closer and more qualified to reach him before me.

Every one appeared frozen as I got to him to see that he was completely motionless. I told him I didn't know if he could hear me, but he wasn't alone. I searched for his pulse beneath his dirty flannel shirt. I guessed him to be in his sixties.

The only thing I felt was the pounding of my own heart as I surveyed the scene. He had been riding a bicycle and was struck by the SUV. He lay motionless, face down, with his legs somewhat askew.

I debated flipping him over for CPR versus risking a spinal injury. I decided that breathing was a little more of a priority than mobility, and I would move him if I had to.

All of this happened in probably sixty seconds or less but felt like a slow-motion movie. I placed my hand on his back to try and feel respirations. He let out a long, loud breath of air, and I began to pray for him. He exhaled loudly one more time, and I feared it was the end. I had heard sounds similar in hospice.

Then he took a deep breath *in*. As I continued praying, he became more and more alert, and began saying "Thank you, Jesus" and "Amen."

He didn't know where he was or what happened, or even his name. But as I told him to hang on, that God was with him, that God saved him for a purpose, he began giving praise. There was some blood, but his injuries were not obvious to me other than he never moved his torso or legs.

I held his head until EMS arrived. They took over with quick precision.

The man that hit him had already collided with a car, lost a wheel, traveling out of control until he hit the man on the bike, dragging him over one hundred feet, and running over him with both tires.

After it was all over, and I lay in bed that night, I thought about how many wounded and brokenhearted people are out there, run over by life, the wind knocked from them.

How many lay motionless as others look on but fail to help. I will say that those that had witnessed the accident were in shock and that they didn't believe the man could live through what they just saw.

How many lay there bleeding as others bend over and look on, failing to assist, and shocked at the sight of pain and wreckage before them. Sometimes, we spew euphemisms or scriptures to those on the ground (maybe that was just me) when what they need is our hands on their back as we reassure them they are *not alone*. That he is with them, and help is on the way. We stay with them while they exhale all of the painful, stale air life has knocked from them. We pray for them as they inhale *his love* and *his grace*.

We hold their broken bodies because someone once held ours. We realize and understand we are called to heal and bind up the wounded and broken hearted, using the healing ointment of his great love, the gauze of his grace.

I don't know if I will ever see Ray again on this side of heaven. I just know for a moment heaven invaded earth as I felt the power of the great physician, and his overwhelming love for that man laying there.

He has it for you, and for all around you. Exhale. Inhale. Repeat.

And—pray for Ray. Who is Ray? I am Ray. You are Ray, and our wounded brothers and sisters are Ray.

Chapter 4

Growing up, she said some very hurtful things to me as I was her brother's "stepchild." As the years went by, she racked up offense after offense, all the way up to a couple of years ago, when she announced at my kitchen table that my sister was always "her favorite."

We had moments throughout the years when I saw glimpses of someone different than the bitter woman before me, but most often, it was only bitterness and pride reflected in her eyes.

Time did what time does, and she became ill. My dad and most of her other siblings had already passed away as she neared the end of this life.

I went to see her in the nursing home before she passed away. I saw a little girl lying in a big bed, and wondered for the thousandth time what had caused her such bitterness. I told her I loved her, silently forgave her, and prayed with her.

She crossed over, and now I found myself preparing to do her funeral.

What? The very one that had said this and that to me? How to memorialize someone that had been so unkind to me was a daunting task.

As I prepared and prayed, revelation about bitterness was given to me. What I found was *not* her bitterness, but my *own*.

I held those painful encounters with her close to my heart, never releasing her or myself from them. I recounted them over and over when I would excuse myself from stopping by her house though I passed it thousands of times.

The bitterness and pride that I always saw was my *own* reflection. I walked in such hypocrisy, professing to possess the unconditional love of Christ, yet not lavishing it upon one who was right before me.

After much time in repentance and prayer, I received the message for her funeral. I was able to stand before my family with a pure heart, chastised beyond measure for my own sin.

It's so easy to forgive Jo Blow—yet we hold such grudges with our own family. We give ourselves the "right" as we stand in our own stiff-necked pride—"If you only knew what they have said/done to me, you would understand."

No. Just . . . NO. Release *them*. Release *yourself*. When we recount the pain and wear it like a Boy Scout badge, a root of bitterness is formed. What will grow from that is only *more* bitterness.

Who has wronged you? When you look into their eyes, make sure that what you are seeing is *not* your own reflection as it was with me.

In heaven, every relationship is made perfect. What was broken here is not broken there. We can bring heaven to earth though. It is but one-bended knee and whispered confession away.

Forgive them. Forgive *you*. I cannot go back and visit her any-more. I can't undo what has been done. I still pass her house all the time, and every single time I feel an ever-growing love and longing that cannot be fulfilled on this earth. I am aware of opportunities and memories missed because of my pride and bitterness.

I have been forgiven, and I forgive myself, so there is no condemnation, only a conviction to love harder.

And I keep a watchful eye out when a friend or loved one "ticks me off." I try to release them immediately to save myself from the prison of "me."

One fine day, she and I will walk together. Visits missed will be made up for in eternity. All of her pain and my pain will be washed away in the sea of forgetfulness.

Want to be happy? Get into the sea of forgetfulness here, now. Start with your own family and yourself. Forgive. Love.

I am in awe that I had the honor of doing her service. What will people say at yours? Our headstones will have our date of birth, and date of death with a dash in between.

The only thing that matters here is what we *do* with that dash. Do the dash in *love*!

Chapter 5

My mind was thinking about my latest hospice patient as I drove to the family farm to meet her. Suddenly, I slammed on my breaks, halting just before the lady bent over the dog.

The dog. I have never seen injuries like that in my life. He had been run over and had several compound fractures.

Bits of bone with flesh were hanging where his foot used to be; his foot now dangling by a tendon or two only.

He was a German shepherd and was so gentle despite his injuries. The lady and I tried to figure out how to get him in the back of her truck with the least amount of additional trauma. Traffic was now stopped around us, and it seemed time was as well.

There was a vet one mile away. We carried him in, and they took us right into a room. The vet came in and surveyed his multitude of injuries. The lady offered to pay for any and all treatment that the dog might need.

After a brief examination, he told us that the dog wounds were too extensive; all of his legs would need to be amputated. The best option for the dog was to send him on into a peaceful slumber.

We both stood there in shock and sadness. We knew it was the best thing for the poor animal, but that didn't keep the tears from flowing.

We both said goodbye to the sweet boy as his eyes looked into ours with a knowing and a peace not of this world.

The lady and I hugged out in the parking lot, two strangers brought together over a wounded animal in our path.

I left somewhat in a daze. By the time I arrived at my new patient's house, I had my emotions back under control.

Actually, it wasn't her house. It was her daughter's home. My patient, "Betty," had lived out west until the week before.

She had cancer, and her husband of four decades was unable and unwilling to care for her. He was consumed with alcoholism. She now found herself 1,200 miles away as she faced the end of her life with a broken heart in addition to her failing body.

Her story broke my heart. We discovered we shared the same birthday, and were both voracious readers. Despite our conversation, I saw resignation in her eyes. I saw that same peace and letting go that I had seen in the German shepherds eyes an hour before. Two very wounded beings, with a *peace* given not of this world.

Life is *precious*. People are broken and wounded. Hear their stories, carry them to help.

I know that ole dog found peace, and I know that sweet lady found peace; all despite the horror of what it looked like.

It was days like this day, where I truly learned of his strength as my own knees wanted to buckle. All of my Christian cliques failed me; all of my knowledge of how God operates escaped me.

I learned that even in horror, I could feel the holy as he taught me over and over the verse, "My ways are not your ways."

Who could I blame for the German shepherd? The one that hit him and left the scene? The owner that didn't secure him properly?

And Betty—who to blame for her pain? Her husband, that in his own illness, failed to show her the love and commitment that is "till death do us part?" The alcohol that stole from their lives and their end days?

There was no rhyme or reason, some blame, and some fault available to be assigned. But above the blame and trying to explain the unexplainable, there was some beautiful hope that danced around, and through my soul, singing of a great plan and peace to trust it.

The wounded animals and the Betties of this world are all under the watchful eye of a loving God, working all of those things together for good.

Their *good* and our *good*. No matter how rough it looks right now, hang on. He kinda has a *plan*.

Chapter 6

While it's a story in and of itself, I found myself walking down the highway one night in a thunderstorm. I walked to my friend Tammi's house. As I walked down her road, I had never felt more alone or desolate. The lightning flashed and the thunder boomed, reverberating through my being.

I cried and I prayed as I walked, and an overwhelming presence and peace fell upon me.

I heard a noise, and a horse had run up to the fence. As I walked, the horse looked at me and walked down that fence row with me. I had never felt anything like it. It felt as if that horse could see into my broken soul, and with his gentle eyes, he let me know I was not alone.

I knocked on Tammi's door, and for the first time in my life, asked another person for help.

I told Tammi about the horse next to her house and the overwhelming peace and presence I felt as he walked with me. We both knew that God had given me a gift.

Fast forward—many months down the road, I was working at the country club, when Tammi's husband, James, came and told me that there had been an accident. Tammi's younger sister had been in a car wreck at the Dam. She was being life-flighted.

We raced home, and I picked up Tammi to take her to the hospital in Tulsa. Halfway there, she received the devastating call that her sister did not make it. It was heartbreaking as we drove, and my best friend's heart was shattered.

A day or two later, I bought Tammi's niece a sketch pad and some pencils. She was nine years old and had just lost her mother. I had only met her couple of times, but something led me to stop and get her art supplies. Perhaps it was because I had been drawing a lot of my pain as words had failed me during this time.

When I got back to Tammi's house, I showed her what I had bought for her niece, asking if she thought it was Okay. Tammi told me that she *loved* to draw, and we both took comfort knowing that God directs our steps, even when we haven't a clue.

Her niece came over, and I gave her the sketch pad and pencils. She thanked me and sat right down to draw at the kitchen counter.

Tammi and I busied ourselves, and then came over to the counter to see her nieces' picture.

She was an *amazing* artist. She had drawn the horse and fence from next door. The horse. She had titled the picture, "The horse by my Aunt Tammi's house." Tammi's eyes met mine, and we both felt the holiness of *that* moment descend upon us.

She could have drawn a million other things—but she didn't.

The same God that had brought me peace and let me know his presence was with me, using *that* horse, was the *same* God in Tammi's kitchen.

He wrapped his arms around *her* and her family during their dark, rainy night of grief, just as he had done for me on mine.

He is a *big* God. When he tells us to seek him, and we shall find him, he means it. And often, it's in the unlikeliest of places. Like a gentle giant of a horse walking down a fence row or appearing on the pages of a broken-hearted little girl's sketch pad. But—have no doubt. He is *present*.

Chapter 7

I had a patient on the outskirts of town that I loved to visit. We would sit on his back porch as he smoked fat cigars and told me stories. He took a quick turn for the worse, and was put in the nursing home, where he quickly became nonresponsive.

I received the request for the chaplain to come. I walked into his room and found him surrounded by his family, our social worker, and nurse.

They all cleared a path for me to come to the side of his bed and lead them in prayer. The room was eerily silent, everyone speaking in hushed tones. He had been unresponsive for some time. I sat down on the edge of his bed and he immediately sat up, screaming. For just a moment, it seemed like a miracle!

It took only a split second to realize that I had *sat* on his catheter!

The nurse took care of his "discomfort," and he drifted back into peaceful unconsciousness.

I was horrified, but the family actually laughed about it after it was all said and done. Almost two years later, I was speaking at a church when the daughter came up and laughingly recounted that story, asking if I remembered—oh yes, I remembered!

God keeps me humble.

Chapter 8

I surveyed the tangle of weeds and ground cover before me. Sweet honeysuckle mixed with ugly thorny vines, poison ivy mixed with Velvety Purple Irises.

Before I began, my eyes travelled over to my neighbor's place.

Geesh, what a mess!

Trash was lying about, scattered among the supposed treasures of his latest flea market binge. How was I supposed to concentrate on my place when his place was such a mess?

I decided I should go over and talk to him about his mess. Maybe give him some pointers and let him know that his mess has not gone unnoticed. Of course I didn't have time to help him clean it up as I am far too busy.

And that, my friends, is how I used to live the Christian life, always seeing my neighbor's mess instead of dealing with my own.

It's so much easier to sit back in judgment when you survey someone else's "yard." However, God is calling us *out* of that place.

He is calling us to a place where we separate our own honeysuckle from poison ivy.

The honeysuckle is the Kingdom of Heaven and all things thereof, relating to *love*. The thorns are the cares and lies of this world that have been sown into our lives.

The thorns prick us, and we, in turn, prick others. The day has come to pull those things out by the root. I don't have to pull my neighbors, just my own.

And I can do none of it without the power of the Holy Spirit.

The awesome thing is when I do get my "yard" tamed, I then get to help my neighbor, from a place of humility and love (instead of judgment), tame their yard.

"Remove the log from your own eye, so you may see *clearly* to help your neighbor with their speck."

Logs and specks impair our ability to behold Jesus.

Once my logs are gone and my yard is clean, I get to help others. But it's not a one-time deal. Storms come, new things grow and fall in my yard, and constant maintenance is required.

When you set your eyes on your own yard and begin clean up, you'll find you don't have the time or energy to judge your neighbor's yard anymore.

Now, I think I am going to suck on some sweet honeysuckle as I cut away the thorns. May as well celebrate the process.

Chapter 9

When I first met Coach, I fell in love with his surly attitude. And—I was heartbroken for him. He and his wife had both entered the nursing home together in June. Shortly after, he was diagnosed terminal and placed on hospice care.

Then—his wife died unexpectedly. They had two sons, and it was so sad that they had just received the news of their dad's terminal diagnosis, and then lost their mother on top of that.

Then—one of the two sons was hospitalized, and died suddenly of pneumonia. It was *so terrible*!

We had to tell Coach that his son died . . . all of this happened in two months' time. He had just lost his wife, and now his son, and was facing his own pending death. And—his son had just lost his mother, his only brother, and was facing losing his dad. It was truly the most grief I had ever experienced.

We told Coach about his son . . . after some denial, then tears, he looked at me and said, "*You* take care of him" and pointed to his heartbroken son. I assured him that I would but more importantly, God would.

We were able to get Coach out of the nursing home to attend his son's funeral. The dirt was still fresh from his wife's grave.

Just a month or so later, I received the call that Coach was crashing. It was late at night. I got to the nursing home, and within minutes of arriving, Coach slipped away.

His son and I went outside. We had already had very long talks before this day. His grief was overwhelming; he had no wife or children. He felt very lost and alone.

As we stood outside, a gentle rain began to fall. He began to cry and shake his head back and forth. I hugged him, and he said, through his tears, "No, you don't understand—Daddy loved the rain more than anything on this earth!"

Wow. The holiness of that moment eclipsed the weight of all that death and grief! God knew exactly how to comfort that son's heart. We both stood there, with our faces upturned to the heavens as the gentle rain washed us both of the pain and earthly sorrow.

That moment strengthened him for the coming days. As I sat with him at Coach's funeral, with his mother and his brother's graves both still fresh, he had a peace that can only come from above.

His face and soul were still wet with the reality of life beyond the grave and a heavenly father that loved him enough to match his tears with loving rain.

"Come to *me*, all you that are weary and heavy laden, and I will give you rest."

It's true. I saw it and felt it in the parking lot of a nursing home as heaven opened up and showered a broken man, bringing him peace when there was no earthly way to have it.

Let it rain.

Chapter 10

My grandmother was changing before our eyes as dementia claimed more and more of her mind.

Ohhhh—her mind! My grandmother was a brilliant woman, and her wit was razor sharp! When she began "losing it," she said and did some hilarious things.

My mom and dad cared for her, when she could no longer care for herself. One day, as I sat next to her on the couch, my dad walked through the living room.

Grandma pointed at him, and said in a whisper, "You know who that is?" Before I could respond, she said, "It's Crazy Jimmy from the nursing home!"

She was completely serious though she had not spent *one* hour in a nursing home! Our family laughed and laughed, and we began to refer to dad as Crazy Jimmy!

My grandma crossed over, and just a few years later, my dad was diagnosed with lung cancer and placed on hospice care. He was dependent on oxygen and had a huge oxygen tank, four feet tall, in the dining room.

That tank was a constant reminder of the battle this big, strong man was fighting. Cancer can steal so much of your dignity.

So—I did what any loving daughter would do. I got one of my mom's wigs (from her battle against breast cancer), one of my dad's flannel shirts, and his hat. I "dressed" that ugly big oxygen tank and put a sign on him, "Crazy Jimmy."

Crazy Jimmy was a moment of laughter in a sea of pain, sickness, and medical equipment. He stood tall throughout my dad's battle and was a conversation piece for visitors and new hospice people. A diversion from the reality of pending death.

My dad and Crazy Jimmy are both a memory now . . . but as my mom and I laughed about this just yesterday for a moment, we were transported to a time and a place where my grandma and my dad joined us—a place untouched by death—a place of laughter and not taking this life quite so seriously.

Find the humor and laughter in the pain of life—it is there, waiting to be mined from the depths, like a priceless diamond.

Thanks, Crazy Jimmy.

Chapter 11

It was 1998, and I was walking out of the mall in Muskogee. As I walked out, I saw a man sitting against the wall, bedraggled and talking to himself.

I walked past him, on my way to my car, when I clearly heard. "Tell him I love him." This was the very first time I heard "that voice." It wasn't audible, yet it almost took me to my knees with its magnitude and clarity.

Yet I walked on, arguing. "No. He's a crazy person. He'll probably stab me or something!"

"Tell him I love him."

I got to my car, put my purchases inside, and struggled. Over and over, the same words came to me.

Finally, I surrendered. I had no idea how to even approach this man, let alone give him a message "from God." I mean, which one of us would look crazy then?!

I walked over and knelt down in front of the man. He raised his head in shock and uncertainty. I looked him in the eye, and said, "God, told me to tell you that he loves you."

The man began to cry. He cried for a bit and then began to tell me how he had to take lithium for bipolar disorder and felt very crazy and unloved. He thanked me repeatedly, and I will never forget what it felt like to see his whole demeanor change.

I never forgot this encounter. A couple of years ago as my life unraveled and was taking my sanity with it, God put the face of that man before me . . . God told me, "I love you" and then I *knew* that the words he had me tell that "crazy" person twelve years before were *also* for me. If God loved that man in the midst of his "craziness," then he loved me in the midst of *mine*.

Every seed that we sow in love and obedience will produce a harvest in our own lives at an appointed time.

Listen. *Expect* to hear God "My sheep, hear my voice." Will you look crazy? Absolutely. But it's that very voice that led me out of crazy and into peace and a sound mind. And it all started by sharing his love with another *first*.

He is a big God with a big voice. Be still, and listen to him whisper his love to you. Or—to another through you. Either way, it is the voice of love.

Feeling crazy? It's okay. God loves you too.

Chapter 12

Funeral arrangements. That is what my mom, sisters, and I found ourselves making after Thanksgiving. My dad had become mostly nonresponsive, and hospice was walking us through his last days. We went and picked out his casket, and all the other things you never want to think about having to do.

I had just moved back from Nevada, and the day I arrived back in Oklahoma, my dad was diagnosed with lung cancer. Treatments failed, and now we found ourselves here. My house and land were not closing until after Christmas, so I was living with my parents.

It was December 7, a day that lives in infamy. My mom came in and woke me up around midnight, saying my dad was insistent that he wanted to get up. He hadn't moved out of the hospital bed in a month. He went from nonresponsive to saying that, "God healed him, and he wanted to *get up*."

Well, my dad was a *big* man, at 6'3" and 200+ pounds. I came in and began to "reason" with him as often I could talk him down from his morphine trips, etc. He just kept saying God healed him, and he wanted help getting up. I thought he was hallucinating again! I said, "Well, if God healed you, *get up* yourself!" (I've asked forgiveness a million times!) "Lazarus didn't ask for help, he just walked right out of that cave!"

I tried to tell him he would fall, to wait till the morning when we had help with him . . . he looked right at me and said:

"Did Jesus schedule his miracles?" *Bam*!

I helped him to the side of the bed and not only did he stand up, he took several steps just to be a smart-aleck. Oh, the cancer was still there . . . but my dad lived another year and a half. During that time, he began to paint from his hospital bed. He painted over one hundred pictures during that time. As his body deteriorated before our very eyes, his spirit and soul flourished.

His first paintings were illegible. But he didn't *ever* quit. I encouraged him to sign them, and he began painting three white crosses at the bottom of his paintings, inspired by the Randy Travis song, "Three Wooden Crosses."

The day came when we did have to say goodbye. I called the funeral home that hadn't heard back from us in almost two years, and we made an appointment to go in. We had already picked out everything before, but now the casket was no longer available. They showed us the "new" model.

The inside of the new casket was *three crosses*.

God only paints masterpieces. It may look illegible at first, but the end result is *always* breathtaking.

Chapter 13

The sight before me was unnerving. This beautiful wife and mother were being ravaged by the unrelenting disease of Alzheimer's. As she paced about her room, mumbling incoherently and alternately crying, my heart was broken for her.

I flashed to what happened before my visit. I was in my office praying, when I felt led to grab my CD player. As I pulled into the parking lot, I was arguing with the Lord because I had no words of comfort yet and felt wholly inadequate for this task. I had been asked to provide spiritual counseling for her husband, and it had led to this visit with his wife. As I turned off my car, I "saw" a Dennis Jernigan (DJ) CD in my mind. I had several, so I flipped down my visor and carefully selected one.

Sitting in her room, heartbroken, the CD player and CD came back to my mind as my soothing assurances were ineffective against the torment of being trapped in your own mind.

I plugged in the CD player as she paced, stripped, and cried. What happened next was one of the holiest moments I experienced in hospice. After DJ's voice began to fill the dark corners of the room, the dark corners in her mind began to recede . . . within moments, she was sitting on her bed, stilled, soaking in the sounds of worship. Her hands became still in her lap; her eyes took on a different faraway look. We sat together, two women worlds apart, yet brought together for this holy moment of worship of our king.

Death and disease was chased from that room for a space in time as *life* filled every nook and cranny of the room and our souls. I can't tell you how long it lasted; it was a moment and it was an eternity.

I left the room, in awe of God's goodness in giving me that tool.

As I shared the story with her husband outside her room, his eyes immediately filled with tears. He said, "We use to follow Dennis and Melinda Jernigan! We always went to his 'Night of Praise' in the city! We have his CDs at home."

I had no idea.

We both stood there, stunned and aware of the holiness of the moment, when the master of the universe reached out and made it very clear who was really playing the music that we dance to in this life.

Chapter 14

I never celebrated his birthday . . . not that I can remember, anyway. We were less than two years apart, my brother and I.

Mom says he used to pull my hair out and watch it shine in the light. In the beginning, it seemed that Bobby was a healthy baby boy.

Not long into his life, seizures began to wrack his body as tumors began to grow internally and externally. He learned to walk and talk before regressing back to infancy from brain damage.

At just a few years of age, Bobby was hospitalized full time in California. His disease was very rare and few lived. They said Bobby wouldn't reach school-age.

Yet Bobby lived. Year after year, we received yellow envelopes stuffed with medical jargon and little hope. I saw him once when I was seven, then not again until I stared down into his casket more than fifteen years later.

Before he died, my mom flew to California. She got to the hospital and held Bobby, now a man. She stroked him and told him she loved him and it was going to be okay.

My dad insisted my mom leave for lunch. They said that as soon as my mom walked out of the hospital, Bobby took his last breath. He was just waiting for her.

Last year, in New York, I surrendered my life and love to Christ. I resigned to live alone, yet prayed for true love. One night, I drew a picture that had me surrounded by his love. I went to sleep that night and had the most amazing dream. I dreamt that I was in the middle of the most incredible love story and being held and cherished by a wonderful man.

I woke up and was still overwhelmed with the feeling of love. I wrote about it in my journal. A few months later, after my Red Jeep (another story) love story happened, I was head over heels in love!

My bestie asked me if I felt the way I felt in my dream. I was *floored!* I felt exactly like the dream and was in the middle of a beautiful love story!

I looked up my dream in my journal, and I had it on my brother's birthday. It was almost like a gift, telling me to hang on, someone would love me and blow me away.

I may not have celebrated his birthday the first half of my life, but I will the second half. I will honor it as a day God showered me with his love and revelation and honor the life of my brother.

One day, I will thank him for being such a great big brother. Maybe we'll even have birthday cake together.

Chapter 15

Almost exactly two years ago, I was preparing to officiate my second funeral of the week. Both were women that I had never met before. Both were with the same funeral home.

I met with one family Sunday, and performed the funeral Monday morning. On Tuesday, I made an appointment to meet the other family at the funeral home during their loved one's viewing.

I arrived Tuesday evening and visited with the family as they tried to sketch a picture of the last eighty years of this dear ladies' life.

After I went home, studied my notes, and prayed for direction of the Holy Spirit, eagles kept coming to the forefront. She was an avid bird watcher, but had a passion for eagles. I prepared my message for the next morning.

I arrived at the funeral home the next morning. As I gave my "order of service" to the funeral director, he said, almost sheepishly, "*Uhhhh*, the family has another short video they want to play—when do you want to do that?"

Now, if you've ever done a funeral, you know that you have the order in your head, beginning to end. It is such a delicate time that you do everything to be as flawless as you can be.

I took a deep breath, looked over the order, and said, "Just play it after my message and before the closing prayer." The disturbing part was that we had no idea what was on the video as they were already playing a memorial video.

I got up, got out of the way, and God did his thing. Just the week before, my mom had told me about a huge eagle's nest by her friend's house. I had driven out there to see it. I have researched eagles before but brushed up on things that the Holy Spirit led me in.

As I spoke about eagles, the departed, and the glory of Christ, the family kept looking at one another. I summed up my message, and sat down for the playing of the unknown video, a bit apprehensive.

What came on the screen made me catch my breath. It was a three-minute video with music and video and scriptures about eagles.

I know that everyone there—with the exception of the funeral directors, immediate family, and myself—thought that the video purposely punctuated the message.

I was undone by his holiness. The family and I cast glances at one another, communicating in a language not of this earth.

Thank God he had his own agenda. Only he, by his spirit, knows how to reach into the darkness of a grieving heart, piercing it for just a few precious moments of illumination.

He knows how to speak into every heart, and he doesn't need an orderly service or stale rituals to do it. May we all move out of the way and allow him to do his thing in and through us. We hope in him, not us.

Why?

"Because those that hope in the Lord shall renew their strength; they will soar on wings, like eagles; they shall run and not grow weary, they shall walk and not faint."

Chapter 16

I was surrounded by Indians. Literally. It was the summer of my six-teenth year, my second summer without my best friend. I was lost as we had spent all summer, every summer, together. I was in Anadarko, Oklahoma.

A visionary from Oklahoma University developed a summer camp, Explorations in Creativity or EIC. It was a summer camp for gifted and talented Indian students. I was to spend six weeks exploring not only creative writing, but my Indian heritage.

Heritage. Now there's a word. Some synonyms are "legacy, tra-dition, inheritance." The only thing that I knew about my Indian heritage was what I learned in the JOM program at school and from slanted history books.

My biological dad was Cherokee, but I had not seen him since I was a toddler. I was just a few years old when my mom grabbed up her children and barely escaped with her life.

So we really didn't talk about him or my heritage from him at all. In school, I used my stepdad's last name Smith instead of my birth name Hand.

As I found myself surrounded by, what in my mind, were "real" Indians with names like Ginny Tonemah, Bird Runningwater, and

Dode Warrington, I felt even more alienated from my Indian heritage with my last name of Smith. I had never eaten fry bread, been to a powwow, or said the word "aaaaayyyyeeee."

As I said, because of the death of my friend and so many identity issues, at times I felt very alone that summer . . . until—

Sometimes, it just takes a little thing to know that God is in control of the universe and that you are right where you are supposed to be.

One day, while talking to a guy named Sonny (last name escapes me in my old age), we discovered that we had the same birthday. As we continued talking, I was astonished to find that we had been born in the same hospital, on the same day, in California!

Wow! God let me know that I wasn't an impostor. I was right where I was supposed to be—where I belong. And isn't that what we all want, is to belong?

God demonstrated heritage to me. Not the heritage passed to me by my Cherokee Blood, but the heritage because of the blood.

Today, I honor Stuart Tonemah and his vision. I thank him for a summer of exploration and for the friendship of my Indian friends. Pursuing writing that summer was just one of the many beautiful steps of my journey leading to where I am now.

Where am I? Not alone. I belong. Not just to a race of people, but to a God big enough to create the universes, yet personal enough to know when and where a little Indian girl was born.

He knows all your stuff too. And wants you to know that you have a heritage of love, creativity, and community.

Now I think I need some fry bread.

Chapter 17

Two years ago, I prayed every night to not wake up. In the midst of my pain, I was talking to a young man and telling him what his name meant. Then he said, "Since you like words so much, here's one for you—E-N-D-U-R-E."

He didn't know *any* thing about me or *my* story. As usual, I was flapping my gums about God's love for *him* with little revelation myself.

That twenty-something young man inspired by the Holy Spirit, pierced my soul with that word! There have been *many* times that word was like a grappling hook, pulling me from the darkness that tried to consume me.

So much has happened in these two years! I have endured! And— now I thank God for "waking up."

This little room in New York saw many tears as I sifted through the sands of my life, deciding what to cling to, and what to let go back to the ocean floor.

My room was faithful as I tried my hand at things I had only ever hoped to do. It never condemned me for my sobs, and it rejoiced with me through my triumphs.

It held me through my nightmares, and was waiting for the day that dreams would return.

May you all find reasons to *endure* today! It's worth it.

Thank you, little room in New York. I shall never be the same.

Chapter 18

A million years ago, I drove a little Ford Escort GT. It was a cute little five speed. Every morning, on my way to work, I would pass a man at the end of the road, waiting by the highway for his ride to work. And every morning, we shared a passing wave hello. I called him Rideman.

I used to have a very bad habit of putting my makeup on going down the road on my way to work. I mean, that gave me an extra nine minutes of sleep.

One morning, as I flew down that black top road, putting on my makeup, I went off the road a little. I overcorrected, spun in a circle, and went backward up an embankment.

As the car came to a stop, my heart was pounding in my chest. But—I still had to go to work. I threw my little car into first gear, drove down the embankment, and got back onto the road.

All of this happened in sight of Rideman. As I got close, I could see his eyes still widened in shock. I waved hello, nonchalantly, like I did every morning. He slowly raised his hand and waved back.

When I got to work, I saw that I had some branches stuck under my car. Evidence.

Here's the deal. I was doing something I shouldn't have been doing, and someone else could have been hurt besides me. My own irresponsibility led to my wreck. Just as Rideman saw me wreck all those years ago, my friends and family watched me wreck.

I woke up a couple of years ago, and I was once again on that embankment. I was dazed and confused and discovering that I had driven myself to that place.

Just like years ago, I threw it into first gear (gotta start somewhere) and am back on the road. After all, there is work to be done. There were those that stood at the end of my road and saw my wreck, yet still lift their hands to wave. To them, I say thank you.

If you find yourself backward up an embankment today, just throw her in first and get back on the road.

Don't forget to wave like you meant to do it.

Chapter 19

He's only in his late fifties . . . so young . . . was my first thought when I received my latest hospice admit. And his wife was only a few years older than me. I fell in love with both of them from the beginning. He gave me the name Preacher Chick. His room filled up in the nursing home with people playing music—he was, after all, a musician.

I had the honor of being at his bedside when he crossed over. He was surrounded by his beautiful girls, wife, and some friends. His son was serving in the military. I did his funeral, and fell deeper in love with this family. God gave me the message of "Happily Ever After." At his funeral service, I gave his wife a Disney book that went with the message.

His wife and I stayed in touch, as she began to pursue a career in nursing, and walk the lonely path of grief.

Almost one year later, I received a phone call late at night. It was one of their daughters, telling me that their mom had just been killed in a car wreck in Georgia, and she was on her way to the youngest daughter's home to tell her. My heart exploded in a million pieces for them. I threw on some clothes and drove to their home. Gathered, again, were these beautiful daughters, who had just lost *both* of their parents in less than a year.

As I prepared her funeral message, I kept coming back to what she was doing at the time of the accident. She was headed to buy more yarn, to crochet on the road trip back home, when she ran a stop sign and was killed instantly.

Her funeral fell on "Good Friday." I felt at such a loss to bring comfort to this family that had lost so much. God gave me a message, as he always does. Right before I left my house, I felt led to get my son's baby blanket to use as an illustration for my message about the thread of love that God weaves (crochets) throughout our life.

I had preached the message at the funeral home, and was on my way to the cemetery to do the graveside message, when I kept hearing to give the blanket to the middle daughter, Heather. I argued. (Common theme with me, I know). There were other daughters, it was my son's (then seventeen), it still had baby formula on it—all kinds of excuses.

I did the graveside message and over and over—"give the blanket to Heather."

I went to my car, retrieved the blanket, and gave it to Heather. She didn't want to accept it as it was my son's, but I told her it wasn't *my* idea, so she had to.

A couple of weeks later, Heather called me. She was pregnant. She was pregnant (unknowingly) at the time of the funeral.

Wow. It was as if her mom was whispering in my ear, helping the Holy Spirit direct me to give that baby blanket as a sign that God was in control, and weaving together a new, beautiful thing in her life.

I got to perform her wedding with a picture of her mom and dad on a table as they looked over all their children that day.

And—Heather had a son. Of course.

Because God is just that big. He weaves together sorrow and joy to create a beautiful thing from the pain in our life.

And that husband and wife are not "gone" but *live happily ever after*.

Chapter 20

One time I was driving through Amarillo, Texas. It was late at night and pouring down rain. A FedEx truck flew past on the other side of the road. My brother-in-law joked, "I guess it absolutely had to be there overnight."

As soon as he passed by, he had a wreck. We pulled over as quickly as possible and ran back to check on him. It was pitch black outside and the rain was coming down in sheets.

His truck was laying on its side in the ditch. He was unharmed, and already out of his vehicle by the time we were able to reach him. He said a gust of wind must have hit him, but as we had witnessed, he was going way too fast in the storm.

It is the same with us. We have things to "deliver" to other people—smile, an encouraging word, our time, our story, unconditional love—to name just a few.

We must *slow* down in the storms of our life, instead of racing through haphazardly.

Pay attention to the road. Pay attention to the conditions you are traveling in. There are people that need what you have to deliver.

Chapter 21

So there we all were in El-Chico's. A lot of people gathered for a wonderful, heartbreaking cause. Two of my three sons were working that night. My sister ordered something that my son, Jake, had to prepare tableside.

I attempted to take pictures of him, but the pictures didn't turn out—things look blurry, distorted. Unrecognizable.

My life looked like this at one time. I could not see one person or thing that I recognized. It wasn't until I realized that it was I that held the camera that my life began to change.

See, El-Chico's looked like El-Chico's despite the crazy blurry picture. In reality, Jake was standing *right* there, even though you can't see him in the picture. There was nothing wrong with my subject, just something wrong with how I saw it.

I did a few fundamental things wrong when I took this picture, and I had done a few fundamental things wrong when my life was out of focus and blurred.

It's usually the simple things. *Slow down. Take aim. Focus.* And make sure that your subject is worthy of *all* that!

Chapter 22

A chaplain friend of mine asked me to do a funeral as she was unable to.

I got all of the information and made the call to her family. I found myself traveling to Tulsa to meet with them and try to know a woman I had never known.

The story that unfolded before me was heartbreaking. A young son came home from school to find his mother dead. She was only in her early thirties, but she suffered from diabetes, which took her life suddenly.

I talked to her father and her boyfriend in a small house packed with a lifetime of family memories. They shared so many stories of the young woman's love and heart for other people.

As I looked around me, I saw giraffes everywhere. Pictures, small statues, and stuffed animals were tucked here and there all throughout the living room and into the kitchen. She loved giraffes, and her collection reflected many years of accumulating them.

Doing a funeral for someone that you have never met and still bring comfort to the family is a difficult task.

As I prepared the message, I kept seeing those dang giraffes. I began to research them and found a fascinating fact about them. They have a huge heart.

A giraffe's heart is up to two feet long and weighs up to twenty-five pounds.

The message ended up being about this beautiful lady's heart being huge like a giraffe. Like God's. She loved big and story after story illustrated that.

Her family told me after that they loved the giraffe story. I know that to this day, I can't see a giraffe without thinking of that beautiful young mother as I send up silent prayers for her son.

When we remember someone for what they loved and how hard they loved, we can't go wrong.

What will you be remembered for? I hope someday to be remembered for having a giraffe-size heart!

Chapter 23

Twenty-eight years . . . yet it seemed like just yesterday, I lay in this very floor.

My grandma Smith lived right next door to me growing up. I was a "step-granddaughter," yet she never once made me feel any different. She was the first to take me to church.

I would go over on Sunday afternoons and watch "Wild Kingdom" while she busied herself making popcorn on the stove.

I remember the excitement in my belly when I would hear that corn begin to pop!

We would sit and watch Marlin Perkins make Jim do all the dangerous stuff as butter dripped down our fingers.

I remember as she got older and slept more and more, I would hesitate at her door, seeing her head down to her chest in slumber. One of my greatest fears was that I would "find her."

That was not the case. She became very ill suddenly. After a couple weeks in the hospital, they diagnosed her with leukemia and gave her two weeks to two months to live.

We brought her home and began round the clock care. I remember her last, full night—my Aunt Marie and I stayed by her bedside all night, rubbing Oil of Olay on her and wetting her lips. I often thought back to that night as I cared for my dying hospice patients through those long, dark nights.

The next evening, she took the hand of Christ. I remember staring out of the front door just in time to see them bringing her around the corner on the stretcher. They had taken her out the back door.

My best friend had been killed two years before, and now it felt like the rest of my heart was under that blanket.

I wrote a poem for my grandma. One relative suggested I read it at the funeral, but then I was told that it wasn't "proper" because I wasn't *really* family, just a "stepgrandkid."

She had been the only grandma I had really known from three years on. The wound from that burned in me as I sat in her funeral, surrounded by people that were "not really" my family.

Fast forward, twenty-six years later. My sister has raised her children in my grandma's house, and I am preparing to officiate my stepaunt's funeral. We had a rough relationship due to the whole "step" thing, but we found peace and grace in the end.

The very church that I sat in at my grandma's funeral was where I was to perform this service. Also the first church I ever set foot in, at three years old with a woman preacher.

Family gathered before the funeral. I saw cousins and cousins and cousins that I had not seen in forever. As I walked among them, I felt something I had been robbed of feeling before—*connection.*

We all need it. I didn't share one drop of blood with any of those people, yet every single one of them were my family.

As I stood above her casket and preached a message of grace, I was overwhelmed with his grace in "restoring the years the locust had eaten."

I was no longer a "step" anything—except a step closer to wholeness when I realized that families are held together by love not blood. After all, we all bleed red and are truly one family.

The thing your enemy meant for evil, God meant for good. At sixteen, I was crushed at not being able to honor my grandma and feeling stripped of the right to. At forty-two, I spoke over and honored her daughter instead. In the audience was the first pastor I ever laid eyes on. A woman.

God removed a lot of excuses that day. No more loneliness and sorrow for a family that was always mine. No more running from the call because I am a chick.

I am thrilled with my new old family! I thank God for each of them and the memories shared throughout my young years. It was one of those very family members that named me "Motor Mouth" (no idea why) when I was just little bitty. At the funeral, he said, "See? I knew it!" Love him!

Trust God with any and all broken things. Hearts, relationships . . . he has a beautiful plan and purpose you could never begin to understand.

So I'm back in my grandma's floor. But now I play with my great nephew, Carter. I whisper things about Jesus and his love to him.

And the wheel keeps on turning.

Chapter 24

Whether it be grief or divorce, there is no way to process that kind of pain at one time. We could not bear it. So God graciously portions it out, as he provides the mercy to sustain it. We feel free of it, until it is time to let go at a deeper level. Let go of *our* dreams. *our* plans. And know, "For I know the plans I have for you, saith the Lord; not of evil but of good; of a future and a hope." I want to dream *his* dreams, as he painstakingly removes my fingers from the shards of *my* own. My tears wet the soil of my future.

Chapter 25

Summer was a beautiful teenage girl that came to work for me at my childcare center, Jacob's Ladder. She worked in my infant/toddler room and was excellent with the babies.

Her little brother and my youngest son, Joshua, were buddies. Summer took them bowling once, and she had her hands full with those two boys.

Summer had an awesome personality, and a smile that filled any room she walked into. And—she looked like Shakira—just gorgeous. Her parents were great people. Her dad was also my pest control guy, and rescued me twice by coming and removing rattlesnakes—once from in front of the daycare, and two weeks later, from the children's sandbox! He released them into the mountains, though I wanted him to "release" them with a shotgun!

I had sold Jacob's Ladder, and was preparing to move back to Oklahoma. Summer was a senior, and was preparing to be a college cheerleader at the University of Nevada Reno (UNR).

I received the call on a Saturday morning. Summer was a passenger in a car that was street racing in Reno. The car lost control, and she was ejected. She landed over seventy feet away, her head hitting a rock.

Her family wanted me to come and pray with her, and with them as they made that decision no parent should ever have to make. Summer had no brain function, and was on life support.

I was so unprepared for the sight before me. They did not clean her up very much, and the trauma made her look far different than the beautiful girl I knew. I looked at all those machines, doing the work her body could no longer do. I was alone in the room with her, and my mind was having a very difficult time processing.

I had to pray and go to a place other than where I was. A place where there were no machines or blood or swelling or beeping noises— or imagining what happened to her the night before.

As I prayed, I had the overwhelming sense that Summer had "already left the building." As I prayed for her peace, I knew that she already had it. I knew that broken body was not "the end" and could not contain that fiery soul and spirit that was Summer. In short—I knew she *lived*.

I came out and then prayed with and for her family. I was the closest thing that they had to a "pastor." In the same way, her dad came and removed the snakes from my daycare, I came hoping to help remove the fear of the decision they had to make.

There were no words that could take away their anguish and sorrow. But there was a peace that came over us all in that cold hospital corridor as we prayed.

Summer was an organ donor, so they were leaving her on the machines until all that could be done. Her parents took some comfort that, even in death, Summer was giving life.

There are no pat answers or religious phrases that can "fix" people at a time like that. There is only weeping with those that weep. Her parents knew I mourned with them as my tears joined theirs. They also knew that God was in control despite the chaos surrounding them and the broken body of their little girl in that room.

If we do not have faith beyond this world, death is a sad thing indeed. Those parents were given the peace that Heather was in a place of no suffering.

And me? Well, there are many times I have seen someone that looks like Summer, and my breath would catch for a minute. Or as I watched Shakira on *The Voice*, I would imagine Summer as a woman. When the pang of grief hits my heart, I look upward. My eyes lift above that hospital bed and the body in it—to a place where Summer is cheering for all those that knew and loved her.

Her life here was not "cut short." It was transported to a level we cannot even comprehend as she took the hand of Christ and entered a world far better than this one.

I can close my eyes and see her with pom-poms, arms stretched to the heavens and that million-dollar smile! She is but one of many I so look forward to seeing on *the other side*.

Until then, I know that she is cheering for us all—urging us to stick together in faith—as she shouts in encouragement, surrounded by children, full of life, "GO TEAM!"

Chapter 26

A few years ago, I took my boys on a vacation to Nevada and California.

We were camping in the mountains in a place called Twin Lakes. Beautiful, tall pine trees, clear mountain lakes, bears walking lazily on the outskirts of the camps.

We heard about some natural, hot springs a few miles away. Always one for a new adventure, I had to go check them out. I gathered my clan and off we went.

They were awesome. There were several different pools, some in the midst of amazing rock formations. There were several people sitting neck deep in the pools as we walked up.

Well, you know me! I start talking to folks, and am really in the middle of a conversation, when I finally realize that they are all naked. And have been since 1967. And all over the age of 120, I think.

My boys were fifteen, fourteen, and eleven—they were *so* disappointed that we stumbled upon a bunch of naked people in that age group! I grabbed them by the ears, and we kept walking till we found a pool free of nakedness.

Life is full of adventure! Don't miss chances to stumble upon naked geriatric hippies in hot springs!

Chapter 27

Water skiing was the highlight of my childhood summers. My dad would pull us girls all over the lake. Some of the most special times were when my stepsisters would visit from California.

My dad was disabled and had a broken back. Due to his injury, he never skied but was content to pull his six daughters, wife, and various other family members.

One summer, I guess he got talked into it or got caught up in the excitement of it all, but he decided to ski. My mom and a couple of my older sisters were in the boat as me and the others watched from shore.

As my dad untangled the ski rope, it got wrapped around his wrist. He then yells "HOLD it" to my sister who tells my mom driving the boat, "He said 'HIT it!'"

From the shore, he looked like an act from Sea World as he was drug across the lake by his forearm. The water level dropped three feet as he swallowed the lake. As he tried to hold up his hand to show them the rope, my sister says, "He says 'faster!'"

They eventually stopped the boat and the show was over. Dad had a rope burn from his elbow to his wrist, but other than that, his pride was unharmed. He was fluently speaking another language though. French, I believe.

In life, there's a ginormous difference in our father saying "HOLD it" or "HIT it." There have been many times he was telling me to hold it, and I put the hammer down and hit it. Or he told me to "hit it, and I tried to "hold it."

My dad was the one drug around that day, but when I mix up hold it and hit it, I am the one beat up and rope burned.

Your father may be telling you to hold some things and hit some things at the same time.

That's why it's so important to listen—to listen above the noise of the engine of your life, above the lapping waves of your circumstances.

Listen to your father's voice, knowing he will take you on the ride of your life.

Even better than SeaWorld.

Chapter 28

We found ourselves somehow going through the motions of the holiday. The turkey was in the oven, the potatoes bubbling on the stove, and the pies on the countertop, waiting for their cool whip topping.

This year was different, and all of us were trying to pretend that it wasn't. The living room, normally engulfed with chattering children, was swallowed up by a hospital bed. In the bed was my big, strong Marine Corp Daddy. We had begun hospice care, and he now lay mostly unconscious in our midst.

Along with picking out the turkey, we had been to the funeral home and picked out a casket as well. Grief hung over us all as others went about their celebrations.

Time had stopped for us, so it seemed surreal and somewhat cruel that it had not stopped for the rest of the world. The Macy's Parade was still on, football was still being played, and families still laughed around tables.

We thought that to be our "last" thanksgiving with my dad, but in a miraculous turn of events, he lived for another year and a half. We had a Christmas miracle that year as he rose up, briefly, from his hospital bed.

My dad has been in heaven since 2005. This will be our ninth Thanksgiving "without" him.

Many will gather around the table today "without" their loved one . . .

But—are we *really* without them? I know we can't wrap our arms around their neck, but we can wrap our minds around their memory.

We can go to that place and remember their laugh and their life.

Their life has certainly *not* ended, but continues on in a place of absolute joy and peace.

This is not our home. We are all on a journey back to where we came from. Those that have gone before are not missing out on Turkey today. They are feasting on love, and when we remember them and our love for them, we can feast together.

Today, I won't see my dad's empty place at the table. Instead, I will see the addition of his great grandson to our family this year. I know that my dad watches over us all as your loved one watches over you.

Happy Thanksgiving. May it be filled with the love of those around you and the good memories of the ones that have gone before you.

Chapter 29

I only had the chance to visit my patient a couple of times before she left this world. Due to her disease process, she was bedridden and unable to communicate. She departed this world, and her daughter asked me to conduct her funeral. I had only officiated one or two at this point, and they were of patients that I had an opportunity to get to know first.

I felt a little overwhelmed at the task before me. Speaking "last words" over a person's life is an honor, and a huge responsibility. I visited with her daughter. She told me of a woman filled with *life*. I saw a common thread throughout the conversation: her mother's love of dancing.

Her mother would go into schools when she was younger and nursing homes when she was older, teaching them an "Irish Jig." She had danced most of her life, and loved to help others dance.

As I prepared for this funeral, I prayed for God to direct me in bringing him glory and the family comfort. I prayed that this woman, that I had never really known, be honored. I grew increasingly anxious, and felt very incompetent. I kept praying for a message, but nothing was coming.

The night before the funeral, I began hearing the chorus from a song. Over and over and over.

The next morning, we gathered beneath the trees in a little country cemetery in Locust Grove.

I opened the service, read the obituary, and shared a few family stories. I shared a scripture, and then did what I had felt led to do with my heart pounding.

I explained that I had prayed for a message that would honor their loved one's life, and bring them comfort.

I turned on the CD player I had brought with me, and the song that I had heard over and over the night before began to play, the notes drifting above us all.

> I hope you never lose your sense of wonder
> You get your fill to eat but always keep that hunger
> May you never take one single breath for granted
> God forbid love ever leave you empty-handed
> I hope you still feel small when you stand beside the ocean
> Whenever one door closes I hope one more opens
> Promise me that you'll give faith a fighting chance
> And when you get the choice to sit it out or dance
> I hope you dance
> I hope you dance
> I hope you never fear those mountains in the distance
> Never settle for the path of least resistance
> Livin' might mean takin' chances, but they're worth takin'
> Lovin' might be a mistake, but it's worth makin'
> Don't let some Hellbent heart leave you bitter
> When you come close to sellin' out, reconsider
> Give the heavens above more than just a passing glance
> And when you get the choice to sit it out or dance
> I hope you dance
> I hope you dance
> (Time is a wheel in constant motion always rolling us along)
> I hope you dance
> I hope you dance

(Tell me who wants to look back on their years
and wonder, where those years have gone?)
I hope you still feel small when you stand beside the ocean
Whenever one door closes I hope one more opens
Promise me that you'll give faith a fighting chance
And when you get the choice to sit it out or dance
Dance
(Time is a wheel in constant motion always rolling us along)
I hope you dance
I hope you dance
(Tell me who wants to look back on their years
and wonder, where those years have gone?)

All of us listened, and all of us had tears running down our faces. That song and the Holy Spirit wrapped around each of us standing on that little hillside. I did not "preach." I just followed *that voice* as he knows much better than I do what folks need.

I have heard this song twice in the last two days—and it always takes me back to that day, when God used a country singer to preach a message far better than a country preacher could.

On this day and every day.

I hope you dance.

I finally am.

Chapter 30

It was one of the first places that Sean Thomas took me to when we came back to Oklahoma. This quaint little park by Lake Hudson. We would drive through, talk about the different places, and enjoy the sunset over the lake.

I have always loved the lake. My greatest childhood memories happened on a ball field or the lake.

The water has always drawn me. In times of deep depression in my life, I always drove to the lake or to the Dam. And in times of happiness, I went to the water too.

Several years ago, I found myself preparing to do one of my first funerals. The deceased loved to dance and taught schoolchildren and the elderly how to do an Irish Jig until she was into her seventies. The lady I met was far removed from dancing as the disease process had long since confined her feet to a bed, and her mind to another realm.

As I prepared, I kept hearing the song "I Hope You Dance." I've written a story about that day, when a greenhorn preacher stood on a hilltop in Locust Grove, trusting the Holy Spirit as I pushed the Play button on a recorder.

We all wept as the notes drifted out over us, bathing us in renewed hope.

As I said, that was years ago. A few weeks ago, I was meeting Sean in Locust Grove, then following him to look at a place out on the lake for sale.

I pulled into the convenience store where he was waiting, then behind him as we went to check out our future.

As my car went over the hills, I began hearing "I Hope You Dance" in my spirit. I was instantly transported to that day years ago, on that hillside . . . in Locust Grove.

I began to cry as I thought of how far God has brought me since that day surrounded by oak trees. I knew that the place we were going to look at was already ours.

My daddy knows the desires of my heart, and he sings over me. I thought I only played that song for a grieving family, but all these years later, in the same town, God brought it back to me.

So it is with all we do. We believe we are only healing others, when all along we are being healed as we heal.

The place is indeed ours, just a tiny piece of paradise, carved out of love. I've enjoyed the sunrise, the sunset, and now the rain from this lake shore. I must say, they each have their beauty, like the seasons of our life. Whichever season you find yourself in today . . . *I hope you dance* because I sure am.

Chapter 31

It was my dad's last day on this earth. He was laboring for breath as I sat on the side of his hospital bed in the living room. He could barely get it out, but he kept on until he did, "I don't want my children in here."

I assumed he meant only my sisters, to spare *them* the pain—but me? I could handle it, and didn't want to leave him or my mom's side. I mean, I have a cape and matching Wonder Woman panties. However, I honored him and left the room.

A couple of wretched hours went by as the dying process swept through our living room. I was in my parents' bedroom when the hospice nurse told me it was close. I came out to my mom holding his hand, my dad taking a breath only every fifty seconds or so. My mother was sobbing quietly as he slipped away.

I couldn't stand to see my mom in such pain! I went around the bed, got behind her so my dad couldn't "see" me if his eyes opened, and held my mother as her heart was broken in a billion pieces.

What happened next is imprinted on my mind forever. As I held my mom, my dad began to start breathing a little more . . . and all I could hear was:

"HONOR YOUR FATHER" repeatedly. I argued with the Holy Spirit that my mother needed me! Over and over.

"HONOR YOUR FATHER."

So I relinquished my right to save my mom, and got on my hands and knees to crawl around the hospital bed (so he wouldn't see me, which was ridiculous, because he *knew* I was in there!)

I went into the dining room with my sisters. As we all sat there in the pain, one of my sons came to the back door and yelled MOM! I tried to tell him to hold on, but he wouldn't stop.

"Come here! I NEED you!"

Well, that was all a mom needs to hear. I went outside, and as soon as I walked outside, my dad held his arms up in the air and clearly said, "I'm crossing over."

Then, he did!

So today, "Honor you father." When you do that, you'll both "cross over" into beautiful things.

Chapter 32

I was preparing to speak at a dinner for pastors' wives when my friend told me about her. She said she worked with a lady that wanted to help put the dinner together. We were having weekly meetings at my house and one night she came.

She entered my home, checking everything out the way Indians do. I immediately invaded her personal space and welcomed her with an excited hug.

After the event was over, our new friendship continued to grow. During this time, the one I nicknamed IndianChick (Tammi Benge Sawyer) surrendered her third unborn child into the arms of Christ. After her miscarriage, she wanted to go hiking at one of her favorite places in the wilderness around the Illinois River.

When I arrived at her house to pick her up, I saw the depth of this woman's character and the size of her huge heart. She was giving all of her baby things to a lady from church. This lady was getting ready to raise her fourth grandchild as the mother was all strung out. Tammi couldn't bear more children, and in her pain, she blessed someone else.

The lady arrived and picked up all of the items with no clue what it meant to my friend to surrender them.

Tammi took me to a trail that led us to the top of a beautiful hill overlooking the river. We hugged trees and shared our pain. As we were hiking back down the rough trail, a guy sped past us on a bike—I was amazed he could ride on such a vertical, rough trail.

Tammi a.k.a. IndianChick knew the trail through the wilderness. She took me to a beautiful place that I never knew existed. Neither of us could have known that in a short time, IndianChick would be leading me through the wilderness that was my life.

As she pointed me to Christ, over and over, she helped me see things that I had never seen before. She held me as I wept more times than I can count.

In New York, we rode our bikes all over the place. I chuckle as I remember the guy flying past us on a bike on that hill as we hiked down.

May you all be blessed with an IndianChick like mine. With her help, I made it out of that wilderness. I even got to ride my bike on the way out. What a ride.

Chapter 33

I had to blink my eyes a couple of times as it still seemed like a dream. I stared down in amazement at the angelic face of the three-month-old baby girl in my arms.

Her mother, whom I had never met, asked me to "take" her daughter for a little while as her life was filled with drugs and violence. She had left the baby's father, and was living with her girlfriend, when she wasn't sleeping in her car.

She was only nineteen years old. Her mother had dropped off her baby with me at my daycare, Jacob's Ladder, in Nevada, a few weeks before. I had given her my phone number, offering to help her daughter any way that I could.

I never dreamed that it would result in this. I begged the baby's mom to come with me and let me help her get on her feet. She refused and, with tears streaming down her cheeks, begged me to take her daughter.

I did. Isabelle melted my heart the moment that I saw her. Big brown eyes and dark little curls. Her daddy was Hispanic, her mommy was a beautiful blonde, and they made a gorgeous little girl.

Everyone at Jacob's Ladder fell in love with Isabelle. She would suck her thumb and make little bubbles, so we named her "ISABUBBLE."

In a twist to the story, her dad came to live with us instead. He was an illegal alien, and Isabelle's mom told him he had no rights to Isabelle. He was crazy about Isabelle, and almost took off with her to keep her safe.

Instead, he got a full time job and became a really good dad. He turned his life over to Christ, and as he was being baptized in Lake Tahoe, came up smiling, throwing his arms in the air, yelling YES!

I got an attorney and helped Juan protect his daughter. What I couldn't do was get him citizenship. We went to INS and found there was no way other than him going back to Mexico and applying from there.

We were both sickened—if he went back to Mexico, who would protect Isabelle if and when her mother changed her mind? At this time, she was still involved in gangs and drugs in Reno.

Finally, I gave up. I had no idea how to help Juan become a legal citizen, something we both felt was the "right" thing.

Then God did what God does when we give up. I received a phone call from an INS agent. Juan's workplace had been raided and they were deporting all of the illegal workers back to Mexico.

My heart began to race as I stared at the baby girl, now crawling, around my living room floor. I poured out Isabelle's story to the INS agent on the other end of the line. The agent happened to be a woman.

Long story short, within twenty-four hours, I was picking up Juan from INS. They issued him a one-year work visa with the ability for renewal.

What I had spent a couple of months and a lot of worry trying to "fix," God did in *one* day.

What if I had surrendered sooner? *Hmmmn.*

Isabelle was almost two years old when I left Nevada. I gave Juan a vehicle, he had a new apartment, and he and Isabelle's mom were by then sharing custody.

The last I knew, Isabelle's mom was raising her, doing wonderfully. It was a heartbreaking yet beautiful season in my life as I saw the ever faithful hand of God. My mantra during that time, when I began to panic at the thought of "losing" Isabelle was "Trust God, love the baby."

I haven't seen her in over a decade, but I realize that I have never and will never "lose" Isabelle. We never lose Love. Someday, maybe not until eternity, but someday, I will look in those chocolate brown eyes again, and hug my Isabubble.

Never miss a chance to trust God and love a baby, no matter how brief. Love lasts forever.

Chapter 34

I arrived at my new hospice patient's house. My patient was sleeping, so I visited with his wife. As I looked around their living room, my eyes fell upon a picture—it was of a husband and wife that I had just had as patients, and they had both passed on.

It was her mom and stepdad, and now her husband lay in the next room, very close to passing on as well.

In the midst of her grief, she shared a story with me that kept her going.

It was the story of her Italian grandmother. She became very ill, and after some time in the hospital, she was sent home and told she would never walk again.

Eight months later, her grandmother walked into that same doctor's office. He said, "How in the world?!" She replied, "One—aa leeettlle bayyybeee steppa atta time aaa."

This daughter and wife held on to that and I have held onto that as well throughout this journey. If the road you are facing is overwhelming, just remember,

"One—aa leeettlle bayyybeee steppa atta time aaa!"

Chapter 35

It was the fall of 2011 as I walked the shores of Cocoa Beach, Florida, and searched for my way. I was staying with my cousin Faith O'Connor as she has always been inspirational and pivotal in my life. Before I left, I spent some time with all of my family there. For a moment I became so afraid of what was waiting in Oklahoma that I almost stayed in Florida.

While at my Aunt Sharon's house, I perused her bookshelf. She graciously let me take a book home with me, "Why Your Life Sucks and What to Do About It." It was a really good book, yet I failed to finish it anytime soon as I returned to Oklahoma, and after a few months' time returned to the Lions Den one last time.

While there, I finally finished that book. At the end of the book is a poem titled ITHACA.

The very day after I finished that book, I talked to my son Jacob on the phone. He told me how he wanted to go to Chicago and audition for a school, "ITHACA."

I said "What did you just say?!" He repeated it again and I was dumbfounded! I had never heard of Ithaca in my life until the day before. Jacob was speaking of the Liberal Arts School, Ithaca, in Ithaca, New York. The poem that I read, Ithaca, is about going to a new place, and leaving old things behind . . . it's about being free of your monsters unless you choose to bring them to Ithaca with you.

My son auditioned, and was not only selected but given a scholarship for over $40,000/year to Ithaca for theatre arts.

As I finally got free, I found myself moving to New York with my best friends, Tammi and James. James's son and my son "just happened" to be about forty miles apart, 1,200 miles away in Upstate, New York. As Da'Sawyers and I house hunted, God graciously settled us in a space to fit us all. It wasn't for a few days that we even realized the highway sign of the road we lived on.

"Old Ithaca Road."

My son was thirty miles away from me as I began to live life as a strong, brave woman. It was a battle not to bring the monsters to Ithaca, but every single day, with the strength of Christ in me, I won that battle. The girl that picked that book up off of my aunt's shelf just a few years ago, and the girl that God took to Ithaca are two very different people.

So if your life sucks, turn it over, and be prepared to move to Ithaca. No monsters are allowed there.

Chapter 36

Looking at Jack, you would never know that he was terminally ill. He was still a big, strapping man in flannel shirts, blue jeans, and suspenders.

I loved my visits to Jack and Jill's house (not their real names). They had been married for decades, and you felt love and peace the moment you entered their home.

Due to disease, Jack's mind had mostly left him. I say mostly because there were brief seconds of clarity . . . often, Jack could pray and make sense.

Since Jack was still physically strong, he and his disease sometimes overcame Jill and her small frame. He would get out of bed in the middle of the night and become unmanageable. One of their daughters, a nurse, lived on their property and helped during those dark nights.

Jill and her family battled with the decision to choose hospice. Jack seemed somewhat strong in his body though the disease was taking its toll.

They had a trip planned out of state, and Jill asked our opinion at hospice about taking Jack on that trip. We all encouraged her to go.

They went on their trip, and were all in Jack and Jill's RV when their miracle happened. Out of the blue, and for the first time in a very, very long time, Jack began to speak clearly and lucidly.

He told them that he loved them all, but was tired. He told them he loved his life with his family, but wanted to go be with Jesus. The whole thing only lasted about three minutes, but those three minutes broke the shackles of guilt and uncertainty from his wife and family.

They returned home with much more peace than they left with. Our entire team was moved to tears by their story and what God had done for them.

It only takes a few minutes to share your end-of-life wishes with your family. Your significant other should never have to make those decisions that you can make for yourself, now.

Cremation or burial? Do you have or want a living will? What heroic measures are you comfortable/uncomfortable with? For your funeral, what is your favorite scripture/song? Open or closed casket? Statistically, one out of one dies. Make some hard decisions now to save your family the pain of making them for you later.

Jack went Home, and they had two services for him, in two different towns, with hundreds of people at each. He lived and loved, our greatest call. And for a moment, he gave his family the gift of knowing his wishes.

Give your family the gift of knowing yours.

Chapter 37

When I moved to Nevada in 1998, I daily drove past the sign for the Moonlight Bunny Ranch (a famous brothel). Every time I passed it, I felt a burning in my spirit. I had just read Brennan Manning's "The Ragamuffin Gospel," which cited that over 85 percent of prostitutes had been molested in their childhood.

I thought I was supposed to go there and share *my* story and God's Love, but was told "you can't go knock on the door of a whorehouse with a Bible in your hand and think they are going to let you in!" So I waited for God to lead me.

During this time, I wanted to open a home daycare to share Jesus with children. I hoped to have five kids in my living room. I went all over my new neighborhood that had a gazillion children, and didn't get one response.

I also took out my 401K and felt led to put aside $15,000 for God's work, having no idea what that was or why.

I needed to find daycare for my son as I had taken a job at a payroll agency. As I called around, I talked with the owner of a daycare center. As we talked, she shared how she was exhausted from battling breast cancer and wanted to sell her daycare center, "Children's Corner."

My heart began to pound, and my belly began to burn! I asked her the cost, and she told me; she said that she and her husband were willing to carry half the loan, with half down.

Half was $15,000.

By the end of that phone call, I had bought her daycare center. Zero childcare experience, zero idea of how to run a center, just a knowing that it was from *him*.

And it was right across the street from the sign for "The Moonlight Bunny Ranch!" So my discernment was off by about fifteen yards.

There were twelve children when I bought Children's Corner. I changed the name to Jacob's Ladder Christian Childcare and within a year had opened an infant/toddler center and was licensed for seventy-two children.

Through those years, hundreds and hundreds of children passed through those doors as well as many adults that came into a life-saving, life-changing relationship with Christ.

My dream was five kids in my living room; God's reality was countless children on a little street corner in the middle of brothels.

I put a huge sign on the top that said "TRUST JESUS" and a lighted blue cross. I ran into people in the craziest places that told me a story about seeing that sign or that cross and what it did for them.

Jacob's Ladder was an amazing experience, and part of a faithful God's healing hand.

Follow those leadings; listen to *that* voice. And above all,

Dream big. He's a big God.

Chapter 38

Brother Jesse was a really neat black man in a nursing home. Some days, he could hold a conversation, and others, it was just gibberish.

I arrived for my visit to find him in his bed, facing the wall. His eyes were closed, but he was having a conversation:

And the foreign man said, "Ain't got no Ford . . ."
And Jesse said . . . "in heaven" . . . garble garble—and then the foreign man said garble garble . . . and Jesse said . . .

He was playing both parts in this conversation! I listened for a couple minutes, then gently nudged his shoulder, saying,
"Brother Jesse, it's Barbie. I wanted to visit with you for a minute."
Jesse rolled over toward me, never opened his eyes, and said in disgust, "Can't you SEE I'm conductin' business?"
He rolled back over and continued,
The foreign man said . . . then Jesse said, "Ain't got no Fords" . . . then the foreign man said . . .
I listened, chastised for another couple minutes. Thinking I could bring him "back" to reality so we could visit, I nudged him again and said, "Brother Jesse, I just want to pray with you for a minute."

He rolled back over, never opened his eyes, but his face screwed up in aggravation as he said in the most disgusted tone,

"There she GO AGAIN?!" And rolled back to the wall to finish conductin' business.

So I finally got the "hint" and let Brother Jesse and the foreign man finish their deal over a Ford in heaven!

I did mention on the way out though that there are no Fords in Heaven. Only Chevys.

Chapter 39

Tammy was a bigger-than-life teacher I met at Headstart. I was the Childcare Director, and my office was right outside of her classroom.

Of all the teachers, Tammy taught with the most passion that I had seen. I had "God stuff" on my desk, always, and had a "toilet ministry." I always left devotional books in our bathroom. This, along with my conversations, made Tammy label me a "Jesus Freak!"

Tammy and I began to have conversations, and it culminated in her giving her life to Christ in my living room. She became just as passionate about her faith as she was about everything else she did in life.

Time and job changes separated us but never our hearts. We would touch bases occasionally, and always pick up where we left off.

As I did funeral after funeral in hospice, I became weaker and weaker. I left hospice in November of 2010, relieved to be done with death as I have experienced it all of my life. I thanked God for releasing me from death and dying, and my faith was a wreck as my life was just beginning to crumble.

On New Year's Eve, I received a text from Tammy. She told me that her baby died and asked me to do his funeral. My heart was crushed for her and her girls.

I went and visited with Tammy, and went with her to make funeral arrangements—something you should never have to do for your infant son.

As I prepared for Keldrick's funeral, God was sifting what I truly believed. As I had never dealt with the grief in my own life, I ran out of places to run as I prepared to bury a newborn . . . did I truly believe that he lived? I knew theologically that he did, but did I believe that he did?

Tammy and her faith was a witness to me during this time, and after, she thanked God for giving her a son and that he would never have to face the pain that this earth life brings us. Her heavenly perspective and faith blew me away.

Within weeks of Keldrick's funeral, some deep truth was revealed in my life, and like a house of cards, it all fell down. I would see that tiny coffin, and God would hammer in my ears, "WHAT do you BELIEVE?"

As I could run nowhere else, I fell at the feet of Christ. Death after death, all the way to baby Keldrick, God peeled back my theology to give me a faith born in my heart instead of in my head.

They *live*. All those that we say we "Lost"—they are *not*. They are alive in and with Christ.

All those years ago, in my arrogance and ignorance, I thought I led Tammy to Christ. As it turns out, she and Keldrick led me.

Chapter 40

The day started out like any other day at Muskogee County Headstart. I was the Childcare Director and also the person that made sure campuses were always ready for state and fire inspections.

My office was in the front of the building with teacher classrooms up and down both sides, separated only by partitions. When you have over 100 three- to five-year-olds, it's pretty interesting.

Out of the classroom next to mine, I could often hear the teacher, Tammy R. Capps, saying a handful of children's names that were the most "active."

One little boy in particular was all over the place, "Kevin."

"Kevin get off the table!" "Kevin stop running" and many other "Kevin stop."

While he was a handful, he also stood by the door as the other kids arrived, greeting each one heartily as they walked in. "Hi, Katy!" and "Hi, Mason!"

Despite his cheery demeanor, if you saw how Kevin behaved, you would say he was a child that needed discipline. He would end up on someone's status these days as an out of control child.

One day, Kevin's mom dropped him off. He had a mark on his face as his mother told him, "Tell the teacher you fell off the bed,

Kevin." In a monotone, with his head down, he said, "I fell off the bed."

A little bit later, his teacher, Tammy, was helping him in the restroom. He was only three or four years old.

Tammy came and got me. I was completely unprepared for what I saw.

Kevin had bruises on his back from his shoulders to his knees, all different colors from all different times.

Tammy and I both had such a hard time not losing it. I went through the proper channels and DHS arrived to take pictures.

They went before the judge that morning, showed him the pictures, and came back to Headstart to tell us to return Kevin home on the bus at two-thirty.

WHAT!

I stood there in unbelief as the DHS worker told me. I raged, "So is the judge waiting for him to end up on Fox news dead before he does something? Did he *look* at those photos? How can you sleep at night?!"

She looked at me calmly but with empty eyes and said, "You get used to it."

I said, "GOD Forbid!" I wanted to kidnap him, not return him to the same hell.

Oh, the judge ordered parenting classes for the mom's boyfriend that did this. Dear God.

Tammy and I were sick as we put Kevin in line to return home. We were on each side of him, loving on him. I said, "When you are scared or sad, you just talk to Jesus, Kevin!"

Tammy said, "And call 911, Kevin!"

You never know what a child is going through behind closed doors. We thoughtlessly and critically spew out our judgment and two cents about things we know nothing about.

His mother took him out of our care not long after, breaking our hearts.

This story has been on my heart for a couple days. I have thought of Kevin often through these years, sending up silent prayers. In light of all the news recently, may we all have our hearts and eyes and ears open for the "Kevins" of this world. It takes a village, and nothing is closer to the heart of God than these little ones.

Peace and love to you, Kevin, wherever you are.

Chapter 41

Several months ago, my laptop crashed in New York. I can't say I didn't have any warning.

I would be using it, and a warning would appear "low disc space" or "low memory." Not every time, but often and more frequently before "the crash."

I didn't have a lot with me in New York, and I would scroll through hundreds of pictures on my laptop when the pain of missing people became too much.

Some people I needed to miss, and some I needed to stop missing.

See, all those old pictures were taking up *too much* of my memory. I didn't have room for new stuff, nor could I load any new programs because all the old ones were in the way. Also, my operating speed continued to slow down before finally quitting—the "performance" was terrible!

Just as my computer gave me warnings, so did my body and life before it crashed. Looking back, there were a lot of warnings that I needed to delete some things!

God says he wants to do "a new thing." I left no room for him to do that as long as I clung to old programs and old pictures in my life.

When my computer crashed, I instantly knew it was a lesson.

God didn't want me sitting there, crying, going through pictures of a broken life that was no more.

Instead, I had to look to him to download new, life-changing programs that operated properly. I had to lay all those old pictures, filled with pain, down at the foot of the cross and walk away. I had to trust him for new pictures.

So—I began to.

Then an amazing man came into my life! Sean got my laptop fixed for me, so that I may pursue my dream of writing. Already an amazing new memory filled with unselfish love.

The computer dude tried and tried to "recover" things from my hard drive, but said that it was completely fried.

I was not shocked.

So—I have a brand-new hard drive and a brand-new life, to make brand-new pictures and memories with!

Delete the bad, make room for the good! You'll be amazed at how your operating speed and performance change!

"Behold, I do a *new thing*."

Chapter 42

I remember a trip we took in the summer of 1984. We were headed to Los Angeles, California, from our home in Okay, Oklahoma. Now, this was *wayyyy* before MapQuest, GPS, etc. I remember my dad sitting down and planning out his route.

We left and drove across the country, and my dad *never* had to look at that map once. He knew every single left and right turn he needed. He had the route completely planned. It's the same way with our heavenly dad. He truly has already "sat down" and planned out a future and a hope!

As a child, in 1984, I just hopped in the backseat of the car in total trust and faith, knowing my dad had the route planned. And that is the state I wish to dwell in. Complete faith that my dad knows where we are going; so I will hush, hop in the backseat, and let him lead the way.

Chapter 43

It was a Saturday, and I was playing golf when I received the call. One of my patients passed away, and the family wanted me to do her funeral.

I called the family and set up an appointment to meet them the next day, Sunday.

As the family shared personal stories and insights with me, one of the constant themes was their mother's insistence on punctuality. If she said dinner was at 6:00 p.m., you did not eat if you arrived at 6:01 p.m. Story after story through the years of her busting their chops over time.

Well. On Sunday, I took down all the funeral information. On Monday, I wrote it down on our board at hospice. The funeral was set for Tuesday, at 2:00 p.m., I thought.

On Tuesday, I was in my office, typing my order of service at 1:05 p.m. My boss ran in and said, "Barbie! The funeral is at ONE, NOT TWO!"

Aaaaaaaackkkkkkk!

When the family talked to the funeral home, they had to switch the time.

So here I was, *late*—of all people's funeral?! *Ughhh!*

As I sped to the funeral home, I tried to think of which building to crash my car into on the way. Or how to fake a stroke—anything.

I got there, and the funeral was already in process. I literally had to just walk out and begin the message, with about three hundred faces staring back at me.

Only the family knew that I was late. To all the other people, nothing seemed out of order. I kept waiting for lightening to fall from heaven and strike me for being late to Ms. Betty's funeral.

After it was all said and done, the family had a really good laugh. They told me how and when Betty's father died, in the middle of winter with the ground frozen, they put him in the wrong grave. The funeral folks whispered their apologies and the family had a story they told for years!

They thanked me for giving them a new story. I thanked them for their sense of humor!

And Betty—well, I'm pretty sure she is gonna have a talk with me someday! I'll try not to be late.

Chapter 44

I was concerned when I saw his message asking me to call him as soon as I could. We have been friends for almost twenty-five years and he had never asked me to do that.

I finished eating my Mexican food, and went home to call. After a few rings, Richard Merritt picked up. He began to tell me how his pastor had just passed away. He had been the pastor of his church for thirty-five years.

My heart immediately felt compassion and sorrow for my friend and for the congregation. Rick went on to ask if I would come and be a guest speaker some Sunday. He said that he had warned them about me, that you don't know what might come out of my mouth, but that I was led by the Holy Spirit.

I was honored. My first visit to the little white church on the hill felt like home. The handful of people that remained to fellowship was so welcoming that I felt I had been there for years.

Week after week, the kind people asked me back. Now, I am preaching every Sunday and seeing God do wonderful things and bring together beautiful people like Tammi Benge Sawyer and Johnny Armstrong and Eva Mickey Shepherd, among others.

Sonny Puckett was the pastor of Liberty Community. There isn't a moment when I'm not conscious of respecting him and the work he began at Liberty.

Yesterday at church, we decided to have our dinner and fellowship that had been snowed out last week. One of the sweet ladies in the church asked me to read my poem that I had mentioned previously but never read.

I asked Tammi for her iPad so I could read it from there. That wasn't an option, so I was going to just blow it off. Tammi said, "That lady specifically asked you to read it, you should read it!"

"Okay, Okay!" I read, "Past the Pecan Tree" last night, for the first time in front of people. I had no idea how emotional it was going to be. I had a hard time finishing though Tammi assured me you couldn't tell.

My poem is my story, and it centers around a dream I had on April 17, 2011, that came to pass on April 17, 2012, after the crossing over of Kambrin Sophie Grace Dennis.

After I finished the poem last night, a lady turned to my friend Rick and said, "April 17! I can't believe she just said April 17." Rick just shook his head and said "Yeah, I know."

The lady, Valerie, turned to me and said, "April 17 was the day our pastor, Sonny, got *saved!* He said it every Sunday, 'On April 17, 1972, the Lord Saved me.'"

Wow. I was blown away at God's beautiful symmetry. Only he can weave together such perfection and "coincidence."

I don't know what God is up to, having such a foolish woman as myself pastoring. I will, however, go wherever he leads, and thank him that he is orchestrating a beautiful symphony of events, culminating to bring him all glory and honor and praise.

Sonny was saved April 17. So was I. Last year I stood on a mountaintop in New York making a living tribute video. This year, the Lord is working out the details, but I plan to stand on the mountaintop of his purpose on April 17, and celebrate life!

Pretty sure Sonny will be smiling down upon us.

Chapter 45

We were on vacation in Minnesota, having some down time. My three boys and I were snuggled together on a love seat watching *Little House on the Prairie*.

I grew up on "Little House" and have read all of the books by Laura Ingalls Wilder. The morals and messages of Little House are invaluable.

In this particular episode, it was Christmas. They were all making preparations, but ended up snowed in with a blizzard raging outside.

Mary and Laura were going to wake up without *any* presents from Santa or anyone else!

We watch as Mr. Edwards saves the day and delivers Christmas despite the deadly storm. Mary and Laura wake up to their gifts . . .

An apple, a shiny tin cup, and a candy cane. That's *it*. The household was filled with merriment and gratitude as they held their shiny cups to the light and danced around with their candy canes.

Seeing a teaching moment, I turned to my boys and said, "What would you do if Santa brought you a shiny cup, an apple, and a candy cane?"

Hoping they would say, "We would be ever so grateful and just happy to be with family, Mom."

I waited for a split second before Nick, then about seven years old, said—"I would give Santa a piece of my mind, that's what I would do!" Yup, that's *muh boy*!

—with Nick Daniel.

Chapter 46

I went into one of my favorite stores, and hoped I would see her. I did. I have known her all of my life and had not looked upon her sweet face since moving to New York.

I found her working in an aisle. I walked up and touched her on the shoulder. She turned, and we embraced one another in a warm hug.

I hesitated for only a moment and then only because she was at work, and I knew it would be tough.

I said, "I am so, so sorry about your son . . . there are just no words . . ." Her eyes filled with tears as she said, "No, no there's not." Her son was tragically killed this summer.

She said, "What are you doing now, Barbie?"

And for the first time, in faith, I said "Actually, I'm writing a book." I have struggled so much with not having a "job" before coming to this place of knowing I am doing what God would have me do. I said it without the fear of judgment and the unbelief in other people's eyes.

She said, "Well, I want a copy." Her confidence warmed me to my toes. I assured her that I would give her one, and we parted ways.

I went into the bathroom a few minutes later, and she came in, crying, and began to dry her eyes. After she gathered herself, she said, "So what is your book about?"

I hesitated for a moment, then looked in her eyes filled with sorrow and tears, and said, "Grief."

Our eyes locked for a moment and there was an exchange of love and understanding.

She said again, "Please, get me a copy."

Now, I am more determined than ever. I thank God for this meeting this morning and a renewed knowledge that there are so many wounded and brokenhearted people. I recognize them instantly as I am one. I pray that the valley he has walked me through will bring comfort to others.

Who am I? No one. It is not about me. It's about him and the fact that he is near to those with a broken heart.

He healed and bound up my wounded and broken heart. Now, I turn with bandages in my hand for my brothers and sisters. And thank him for bathroom meetings of the heart.

Chapter 47

The long cold winter had said it's goodbyes. Spring had sprung, and now the promise of Summer lay before me.

As a hospice chaplain, many hours were spent in the artificial lights of a nursing facility filled with the sounds of life and death. There may be cake and birthday festivities in one hall, and funeral home guys in another.

The days that I had home visits to make brought some relief, even as the uncertainty of having words of comfort brought anxiety. Some days the long drive to a patient's home provided the quiet time to become still.

This day was no exception. I drove through the windy roads, up and down huge hills as my car hugged the pavement. I was headed to Stillwell, Oklahoma, to meet my new home patient. She was being cared for by her husband at home.

Strawberries were in season and the Stillwell Strawberry Festival was in full bloom.

After almost an hour, my car came to rest in front of a modest white house with flowers dotting the landscape here and there. I walked up and rang the buzzer. As I admired the beauty of the day, I prayed for direction.

The sweetest elderly little man came to the door. He ushered me in to the kitchen, where he was trying to convince his wife to put her pants on.

As I entered the room and their life, I was saddened and angered anew at death and disease. Before me was a wild-eyed woman, clad in a long sleeve shirt and an adult diaper. She argued nonsensically as she kicked her legs like a toddler, avoiding getting dressed.

I began to help as his soft voice began to reassure her that it was all going to be Okay, she was safe.

Eventually we were able to get her britches on her. He led her gently to the "sitting room" and eased them both down onto a sofa.

She began to tell me stories as she calmed down. Because of her disease process, her story was a word salad almost—

"We didn't garble garble fishing garble garble . . ." I would pick out words to build on in an attempt at conversation. As she talked, her husband held her hand, and gazed at her with eyes that held decades of love and shared stories.

I saw something else there in his eyes. I saw a deep, piercing sadness. I knew that he would trade places with his beloved in a moment if he could. I saw the powerlessness that is present when the power is calling home one of his children.

As she talked, she became more anxious. He began to gently pat her as he held her hand. She calmed. It was one of the most beautiful things I have ever seen.

I had prayed for words of comfort but found myself speechless. I had prayed to share his love, and in the way only he can, he shared it with *me* through this gentleman.

They were at peace together, this little man and wife. A love bigger and stronger than any disease bound them together.

I left my heart filled. I stopped at a roadside stand, and bought a bright box of strawberries, thankful for the summer fruit.

Strawberries aren't always in season, but love is. I tasted them both that day.

Chapter 48

Sean and I took Lucy, our cocker spaniel for a walk. I was holding her leash but not really making her heel at all. She kept crossing back and forth in front of me, tripping me and making me stop. Makes walking not nearly as beneficial as, well, walking.

Near the end of our walk, a car came. We got out of the road, but Lucy began to flip out, zigzagging crazily and shaking.

See, in New York, she was run over by a car. That, combined with being a "country dog," makes her panic around moving vehicles.

Sean took the leash from me, and jerked her up short. He gave her no slack, and just kept walking, making her heel. She did. Lagging behind her, I felt kind of sorry for her, having to keep in step instead of having a little freedom.

We began to jog, and another car came. Lucy began to flip out, but Sean just kept running, saying, "Come on, Lucy." Lucy bucked and jerked, flipping back and forth.

I stopped running and started trying to soothe Lucy, angry that Sean just kept going instead of stopping to comfort her and give her a minute.

I knew *exactly* what Lucy was feeling—the panic that takes your breath away and consumes you, because you are suddenly reminded of trauma. Your mind gets trapped and you are there again, pulse pounding and fear coursing through your veins.

Lucy was with me through the violence. That is when she began shaking, long before being struck by a car. She would shake and run to me, or hide when I was being abused as violence filled my home. She still shakes around any new man and raised voices. In short, my dog has PTSD too.

Sean and I finished our walk. I was quiet and huffy, sending mean mental messages about dragging my precious baby that has been through so much.

We talked it out because that is what a true relationship does. Hash out the hard stuff.

As we did, my perspective changed *completely*. I thought he was being insensitive. I was so wrong.

He told me that he just kept running so that she would too. That she couldn't keep freaking out every time she saw a car, that she had to . . . are you ready?

Get past it.

She had to keep moving, instead of flipping out, and endangering herself. She couldn't stay stuck in the trauma forever as a victim. At some point, she has to learn to not let those old things stop her from running today. Just like me.

Sean's wisdom superseded mine. (*Sshhhh*, don't tell him *please*, he'll be insufferable!) I gave her slack, making the journey more difficult for all of us, and not nearly as pleasurable as it could be.

Sean kept her in step, leash shortened, at his side, and she remembered her place. Beside him, she was safer and happier. What I thought was a lack of freedom was actually what allowed her to be safe and, thus, free.

It is the same with God. When I ran ahead and zigzagged in panic, he *lovingly* pulled me up short. He taught me to walk beside *him*, *in him*. The last three years the holy spirit whispered, "Just keep running." Okay, actually it was "just keep swimming" in the voice of my cousin Faith O'Connor and Dory from "Finding Nemo." But for the purpose of this story, it's running!

Many times I was reminded of what hurt me, and began to flip out. Every time that I did, there was tension on my "leash" with God. Just as a shepherd lovingly draws his lamb back by using the rod to *direct* (read: not beat) the lamb to safe pasture, he brought me back to freedom.

My dog has to get past her past. As do we all. She and I have been through hell and back together. Now we are both loved and adored by the most amazing man, given us as such a gift of kindness, compassion, and wisdom.

We will keep running. Lucy will stay in step with her master, and I will stay in step with mine. I'll let Sean hold Lucy's leash, and the holy spirit can hold mine.

Just keep running!

Chapter 49

One I can explain away to myself a thousand ways. I could even find grace from some folk for one. But two? No way. In the "unforgivable" zone for sure.

What "good Christian girl" gets divorced once, much less twice? I found a way to avoid accountability to myself the first time. The second time, I had to see what part was mine.

Oh, not because I was on a journey to have all of my "vain imaginations" destroyed on purpose. I was on a truth-seeking journey though. I Just didn't know I had to face my own along the way.

The Holy Spirit revealed me to *me*. Thankfully, it was as beautiful as it was painful. One week before I walked away from the dark and exactly one week before my car wreck, I heard "Man in the Mirror" by Michael Jackson in my spirit. My mom and I just had lunch when I began to belt it out by the car.

I always wanted to save the world. Truly, I had to know the truth of my own Salvation. Exactly what Jesus was setting me free from. I fell on my face throughout, in awe of his holiness, and my own sin and degradation.

He never left me on my face. Like the woman caught in adultery, it was just he and I as my accusers no longer mattered. I accused myself enough for everybody. And the accuser of the brethren is alive and active as he whispers my deepest fears and flaws to me.

But not Jesus. He put his hand beneath my chin, lifting my face from the dust of a shattered life. He held me there as my eyes met his trembling at what I might find there. His eyes searched my heart, and he poured his blood and mercy and grace and forgiveness into *every* broken piece of it.

Had I not seen his love, I could never have faced and repented of all the times I denied him in my life. It is, after all, the *love* of God that leads us to repentance.

From that place, I painfully began to remove the logs from my own eyes. They had impaired my vision as I judged the world instead of judging myself *first*. After the logs were removed, I then saw my brothers and sisters clearly, and am now able to be close enough that if one has a speck, I can help them remove it.

See, I don't think the logs and specks are particular sins. They are things which impair our ability to behold the lamb, his cross, resurrection, and eternal redemption—of and for us.

So yeah, two divorces. Two piles of ashes. But guess what? That means *two* phoenixes to rise from the ashes . . . or biblically, "I will give you beauty for ashes."

I had so many ashes that I mourned over. Jesus didn't just sweep them away. He asked me for them. It's an exchange. Beauty *for* ashes.

He has stained my two unforgivable divorces and one billion other sins red with his blood. Now, when I behold me, with my logs gone, I see a purity. "Though your sins be like crimson, I shall make them white as snow."

Everybody else sure looks a lot better too.
Search *my* heart, O Lord.
How do we even begin?

I'm starting with the man in the mirror.
I'm asking him to change his ways
And no message could have been any clearer
If you want to make the world a better place
Take a look at yourself, and then make a change.

Thanks, Michael.

Chapter 50

She hurriedly filled out the paperwork before dropping off her son at my childcare, Jacob's Ladder. She looked frazzled as I asked if there was anything else that I could do. She was in a hurry to go to work, so we finished up what we needed to.

That afternoon when she returned, she spilled out some of the pain that was her life. She was in a dangerous, abusive relationship, and exhausted. I offered for her to come and stay with me and get on her feet. She considered and said she thought she could really use the help.

She was supposed to come and stay with me after the weekend. I arrived at work to find a letter stuffed in the gate. She had returned to her boyfriend, apologizing profusely.

I didn't hear from her for a while after that. Then, out of the blue, she contacted me. I once again extended the offer, but told her that I wouldn't again.

"Maria" moved in with her two sons, Pedro and Reno. She became a sister to me as she began to take her life back. She found out that she was pregnant. Thankfully, it wasn't the abusive dudes, it was the father of her second son. He was a good guy, Roberto.

Roberto and Maria reconciled, and he came from California to live with me too. They began to build a family, overcoming the pain and forgiving one another. After a few months, they moved back to California, forging new ground in their faith and their family.

They were married in my living room, and continue to be amazing friends. I drove to California the night their third son was born. They also helped me recently as I walked out of abuse, having told me years before the truth that I couldn't yet face.

There was something very special about Maria. She had a gift. She "knew" things and could "see" things. At the time I owned Jacob's Ladder and was preaching on Sundays in a juvenile detention center. There was a lot of spiritual warfare going on.

Maria told me about my past. Things she could never know. Without getting into sensationalism, many things happened that taught me spiritual warfare on a whole other level when she came to live with me.

She turned her life over to Christ and an intense battle started. She prevailed, and she and Roberto were baptized together, in my church, on Valentine's Day! It was so beautiful to see what God did with the pieces of a broken life. He crafted something precious in the flames, purifying it until it was his kind of love.

Unconditional. Forgiving. Eternal. More powerful than any force of darkness that comes against it.

Maria and Roberto have built a solid home together in California with their sons. The foundation was love, so it still stands today.

Seeing them baptized on Valentine's Day was very powerful. It was a battle all the way to the church.

In my mind's eye, I can still see the water glistening on their skin and in their eyes as they felt the overwhelming grace and love of the greatest Valentine of all.

Chapter 51

People that have known her know her troubled past. Unwanted by the family she was in and sold to strangers in a parking lot. Illness almost claimed her life before she was even a year old; prayers, a good doctor, and a week in ICU saved her little life.

Her home life was filled with violent outbursts and, in the end, she witnessed physical abuse that sent her scurrying to any corner she could find.

My dog Lucy is an overcomer. After freeing ourselves from the prison we were in, we went to New York together. Just before I moved back to Oklahoma, Lucy was run over by a car, but unharmed physically.

The only evidence of her troubled past is when she is frightened. The shaking and quivering begin as her eyes widen in fear and her breathing quickens.

Lucy goes almost everywhere with me. She loves riding in the car, even though she is scared to death by big trucks, overpasses, and bridges.

She will sit in the passenger seat and shake until I let her in my lap. The moment she is in my lap, she begins to calm down as she leans into me. Once she is secure, her favorite thing is to stick her head out of the window and let those long ears flap in the wind.

Me and my dog have a lot in common. Both from troubled beginnings (my mom only *tried* to sell me to strangers in parking lots—ha!), and, we both begin to shake when reminded of the fear or the pain.

I went over bridges and under underpasses as I traveled down this road called my life, yet they lead me nowhere.

I finally understand who belongs in the driver's seat. I surrender all control, just as Lucy does when she hops in the car. I am not, however, content with the passenger seat any more than Lucy is.

Now, my favorite place is in the lap of my master. He knows the way. So I just lean into him until I feel his love and mercy and grace envelop me.

Then, I put my head out of the window, my ears flapping in the breeze, and enjoy the ride.

Chapter 52

I have been trying to conceive since the loss of my last child . . . I just found out that I am twelve weeks pregnant and I am filled with hope and joy once again . . . where is that screaming coming from?

I am on my way home. My wife and I had a huge fight just before I left, so I can't wait to fold her into my arms . . . what's going on?

I just buried my father. I haven't seen him in five years, and the guilt is eating me up. I resolve to go home and call my children, forging new relationships so that . . . please stop the screaming . . .

I'm on my way to ask the woman of my dreams to marry me. A beautiful ring is tucked carefully away, ready to present at just the righ . . . oh God, the screaming . . .

I just got a promotion, and am on my way to training. The salary increase will buy a home for my growing family . . . noooo, ohhhh nooooo . . .

I can't wait to hold my daughter! She just found out that she is pregnant again, after the loss of her firstborn . . . what? what?

My husband and I had a huge fight before he left. Stupid. I can't wait to see his face and tell him how much I lov—what?

My dad just buried his father. Death makes 'ya think. I can't wait to see my dad, and begin a new chapter with hi—what?

I am picking up the man of my dreams. I have hope in my heart that one day we will be husband and wif—what?

I am so proud of my husband. I want to tell him that it's been okay to live in a one-bedroom apartment with two kids because we have each other. I am excited for what our future hol—what?

The above is my fictional account of some of the stories of Malaysia Flight 370. We see the news of heartache and horror every day, and I believe we have grown numb. For every life on that plane, there was a story. I believe that I "liked" a couple FB jokes about finding the flight on Gilligan's Island.

God pricked my heart, and I closed my eyes. I could hear the frightened screams of the passengers, the wailing of family members waiting desperately for *any* news of their loved one.

As far as we know, they rest in a watery grave. May we not see another broadcast of devastating loss of life, and not *feel something*.

Praying for the wounded and broken hearted is part of our call. Feeling their pain is part of our humanity. Let's hang onto both.

Chapter 53

April 17, 2010, I did a conference for Pastors wives in Norman, Oklahoma, "Metamorphosis."

April 17, 2011, I had a dream that I recorded, about helping an abused woman cross a bridge with all of her baggage. I had no idea I was that woman.

April 17, 2012, I began to cross that bridge from death to life. Kambrin Sophie Grace Dennis was taken by the hand of Jesus, and held the key to freeing me from a prison of grief. Thanks Firefly.

April 17, 2013, stood on a mountain in New York with Tammi Benge Sawyer, producing a "Not Church" video and living tribute for Scott Dennis and Lorena Dennis, mentors of my life and faith, parents of Kambrin.

April 17, 2014, I did a first annual "Celebration of Life and Pie" at Liberty Community Church, where I pastor, to honor and celebrate those waiting for us on the other side.

April 28, 2012, I stopped swimming with the shark the night before as I finally walked away from the deadly cycle of abuse. I stood in Tammi's driveway yelling, "I'm awake, I'm alive!"

Hours later, I was rear-ended at a red light, totaling my car, hurting my neck, and breaking my nose.

April 28, 2013, I was in love with my king, living in New York, and searching for my destiny.

April 28, 2014, today. Today. I made it. I crossed that bridge. I get to share the love that saved me as he gives me the desires of my heart. I have my soul mate, Sean Thomas, that I love being loved by. I speak, I write, I do massage.

I taught "Metamorphosis" then I went through it. It's a dark, secret, holy, messy, beautiful process.

It's staggering what God can do in a year with a surrendered life. I didn't surrender because I was holy, I surrendered because I was out of other options, face down in the mess of my life.

If you are in the middle of that dark process, hang in there. The caterpillar turns to a liquid goo in the cocoon. It's that inky blackness and place of seeming nothingness that God is weaving together beautiful wings with thousands of tiny scales. The scales make up their pattern and color just as every experience you've ever had comes together into a beautiful display of the Master's Handiwork.

So yeah. I wanted to give up, but it was worth sticking around for. And as long as I'm already here, I may as well fly and enjoy the view!

Chapter 54

September 14 has always been the date that turned my life upside down, inside out. I have been plagued with nightmares most of my teen years and adult life, mainly about *that* date, and the event that changed my life forever.

My best friend was murdered. His name was Mike Davis . . .

As my life unraveled these last few years, God really pulled back the "curtain" to show me the things I had spent a lifetime running from.

In addition to grief, abuse was there, and he showed me how I ran from abuse, to abuse as it was all I knew.

Death after death, tragedy after tragedy, God was peeling back the layers . . .

In the midst of really bad things happening in my life, Tammi grabbed me on a Friday in 2011 and took me a couple hours away to her sister's house. It was in September, the month I've hated since "that day."

As I walked along a dirt road at her sisters, I began to have "flashbacks" of my teenage years, when I could barely walk to school as I had to pass the house my friend was murdered in. The house I had spent hundreds of nights in.

God showed me all the ways I had run, and then showed me. He gave me the strength every single day to walk that walk.

For the first time in twenty-seven years, I spoke out loud to my friend, sobbing, as I walked down that dirt road far away from home. I told him how sorry I was that we fought that day, sorry I didn't spend that night, and finally, how very much I missed him. As I sobbed, for the first time since 1984, I could feel Mike—feel him tell me it was *okay*. He was *okay*.

Then, I began to remember the good parts of my childhood I spent a lifetime forgetting, because he was in them.

We learned to ride a bike together, play catch together, basketball—all my young years were spent with him. And I had forgotten them all in the horror.

The next day, I went to church in that town far away. As I cried about the state of my life, a lady tapped me on the shoulder and said, "This has never happened to me before, but God keeps telling me to tell you to 'Lay it at the foot of the cross and walk away.'"

I was undone. Those were the *very* words I told others.

I marveled at what God had done on that dirt road and in that church that weekend. It was only as we were leaving town that I looked up at the water tower, and realized the enormity of it all.

I was in Davis, Oklahoma. God is *just* that specific to leave no room to doubt *his power*. He took me to Davis to release me from the pain and grief of Mike Davis. In Davis, I felt the love again from Mike Davis.

This September 14, I am in a new life, with new dreams to dream. And Mike? He lives, and he is nearer than I ever knew.

Lay it at the foot of the cross, and walk away. Lay what, you ask? Everything.

Chapter 55

You could hear her coming before you actually saw her—her contagious laughter or her giving the director of nursing, or anyone else she could a hard time.

She was a CNA in the nursing home. She would bring chicken feet to Mrs. Jones, put corn rows in Mrs. Brown's hair, and she made a nonresponsive patient belly laugh. She was walking sunshine.

When I received the call, I was in shock, along with all those that had worked with her. See, she had this one fault, she took care of every one but herself as so many of us do.

She was murdered, shot point-blank in the bathroom by her boyfriend, who then took his own life. The horror of it swept through the nursing home staff, hospice staff, friends, family, and the community.

I was sent to the nursing home to do grief counseling for the employees and was asked to do her funeral as well as a memorial at the nursing home as there were many staff that would be unable to attend her service.

What no one knew is that my life had been turned upside down by a murder-suicide when I was fourteen years old. This was very "close to home" to me in more ways than even I knew at the time.

I met with her mother and met her four children left behind to grieve a mother they would never get to hug again. It was devastating.

There is no quick answer or handbook for dealing with tragedy. There is only compassion and mourning with those who mourn.

I did her memorial at the nursing home, and as it was almost Valentines Day, focused on how Mimi *loved*. She was also an organ donor, and helped to save five lives in her death.

There were hundreds of people at her funeral. And her funeral just "happened" to be at the same cemetery that I stood in on that horrible day in September, when I was fourteen because of a murder-suicide.

The only thing bigger than the horror of her death was the depth of her *love*. She loved on so many people, and would not be satisfied until she brought forth laughter and a smile from all that she touched.

She gave life beyond just donating her organs, and leaving behind that legacy of *love*. She gave life *to me*.

I began to really research domestic violence and did an in-service at the nursing home, went and visited with the director of the local women's shelter, WISH, and put up a flyer at work.

Almost one year later, to the date, I sat before that same director at WISH. This time, however, I was the one seeking help. As I went through that horrible cycle of abuse and returning to it, Mimi was always just at the edges of my mind. I kept seeing her face, and remembering her fate.

I had almost twenty-six years of grief that I had never had the tools to deal with. As I did funeral after funeral, God stripped away the layers upon layers. Mimi's funeral was a huge part of my "coming undone" and facing the truth of my own life.

As I finally made the choice to get *out* of violence, Mimi's death had even more purpose, and her life was still giving life.

The thing about Mimi that can never be taken, even in death, was her passion and her ability to love.

I'll never forget Mimi, or the freedom I now walk in because of her. I finally dealt with that murder-suicide from all those years ago, and I finally dealt with being a victim of violence.

Now I stand amazed at the hand of God, and how he walked me through the *very* valley I was running so hard from.

We will all leave a legacy when we pass from this world. Mimi left a legacy of *love*, and that is truly the greatest of all things.

I can't wait to hear her laugh again someday. Sometimes, I just have to close my eyes, and it is there. Her life and death helped save me from a life of death and from a tragic end.

The real tragedy in life is not ever living or loving. Do *both*. You never know whose life you will save—it might just be your own.

Chapter 56

I remember it like it was yesterday. We were standing in my sister, Michele's kitchen.

My mom said, "I have something to tell you, but it's going to be okay."

My blood ran cold through my veins. I had had my share of bad news in my life already and knew this was going to be bad news.

Then she uttered the words that way too many people have had to hear.

"I have breast cancer."

It felt as if all the air had been sucked out of the room and out of my lungs. There was complete silence as my sister and I tried to wrap our minds around the words that had just been spoken.

The silence was quickly swallowed up by a thousand questions.

She went for her first mammogram, and they found a tumor in her breast. They were going to operate almost immediately, and perform a radical mastectomy.

I had just begun having my boys, and the thought of losing my mom was terrifying.

Our lives now contained words like mastectomy, lymph nodes, chemotherapy, radiation, prosthesis.

My mom came through her surgery like a *boss* and began the journey of chemotherapy. She continued to work at her job, UPS. I have never seen a tougher woman than my mother.

She never allowed us to see her be anything but positive and somewhat flippant about her battle with that deadly disease.

My mom has been cancer free for almost twenty years now. She would not be with us today if she had not had that mammogram.

October is "Breast Cancer Awareness" month. Ladies, do those self-exams, and schedule a mammogram if appropriate for your age, etc. It takes just a moment of your time, but may save your life and your family a lot of grief.

My mom is a *survivor*. I pray that we would all do whatever we can to make sure that we are too.

Chapter 57

I pulled into Eastgate Manor, preparing to meet my latest admit and family. The only information that I had at the time was a name, Mrs. M.

I walked into the room filled with family. I introduced myself to the patient's spouse and children; my patient was nonresponsive and had been for almost seven years.

She was at the end of a very long journey.

Her spouse, Monty, was quite the intimidating man. The nursing home staff warned me about him—he was fierce! I can't tell you how it happened, but somehow by the end of my one hour visit, he and I were joking together. I asked if I could say a prayer before I left and you could have heard a pin drop. The daughter muttered, "Make it quick."

I did, then gave everyone in the room a big hug as we had all just become old friends.

Well. I went back to my office and the social worker intercepted me.

"Barbie, we have a new admit, Mrs. M, and they've *declined* spiritual services. They are very adamant, so don't even make an initial visit!"

Oops.

So that was the awkward silence I felt at the beginning of that visit! Being clueless, I went in there and just loved on those people. As I got to know Mr. M. "Monty," we became very close.

He told me story after story of religious abuse in his life that had made him bitter of any and all clergy.

He asked me to do his wife's funeral after I sat with them while she passed. It was such a long way from the man that declined a visit.

Several months later, I came into my office, and there was a new admit form on my desk. Monty. My heart stopped for a moment.

Monty and I had a relationship like my dad and I. We joked and laughed and played. And—I prayed. I prayed every visit, and Monty cried during every prayer.

As the time approached, he became unresponsive. His son, Scott, asked me to do his funeral because "I didn't preach at people" at Mrs. M's.

I travelled to Missouri to bury Monty. He dug water wells all over the world for a living.

As I put together the message, I thought about how so many people easily dismissed this grumpy, cantankerous old man. You had to go *deep*, you had to *dig* to find the beautiful heart and soul beneath the surface like a freshwater spring running underground.

Go beyond what you *see* and hear people's stories.

Monty sat by his wife's bedside, every day, all day, for seven years. He fought for her care vigorously. That was the very example that the Holy Spirit gave me to illustrate God's love to Monty, and as time went on, he began to accept it.

I'll never forget Monty or his family; like many others, they became family.

And all because I was bad with paperwork and didn't know I wasn't wanted.

Dig deep, and you'll be surprised what you find—in yourself, and others!

Chapter 58

I was at the nursing home, preparing to visit my latest admit to hospice.

I arrived to find him swallowed up in the whiteness of the sheets surrounding him. Despite his advanced illness, he was completely lucid. His wife of sixty-three years was just as precious as he was.

Mr. C was a fascinating little Indian man. As our visit progressed, he asked me to read a specific passage of scripture.

It was the passage about the lame man asking for silver and gold, outside of the city gates. What the man found instead of earthly riches was eternal life and healing as Peter said, "Silver and gold have I none, but what I have, I give you. In the name of Jesus Christ, rise up and walk." The man rose up.

Well, Mr. C had just recently become bedridden, so this passage spoke to him. Before we prayed, I asked him what he would like to pray about. He looked me in the eye, and with such great intensity and longing that it pierced my heart, he said, "To walk."

I joined him in a prayer of faith, and we prayed that he would walk. I always end my prayers with "nevertheless, thy will be done."

That night, as I was in prayer, and again early the next morning, I had a knowing that Mr. C was to be healed. I absolutely knew that he would walk again that day. I couldn't *wait* to get to the nursing home, pray, and see him walk down the hallways knowing that all would see his healing. What a witness to God's power!

As I drove to work, my cell phone rang. Our social worker said, "Barbie, Mr. C just died. I need you to go to his house to tell his wife, we haven't been able to reach her."

Instantly, my mind filled with denial! I finished the phone call, and immediately burst into tears. I was learning to be more and more honest with my emotions as I cried out to the heavens.

"God! You put that in my heart! And he asked for that scripture about the lame man walking! You said he was supposed to walk *today*!

And a gentle whisper that can crumble the mountains and explode the stars said, "He is."

It didn't look the way I thought it was supposed to look. And so it is with his ways; they are not our ways. I hung my head, humbled and overwhelmed by his holiness and his majesty.

Some day, I will walk by the river with Mr. C. Until then, I'll remember who is on the throne.

Chapter 59

My client was arriving shortly as I busied myself preparing for their appointment. I went out into the hallway, and adjusted the thermostat as it was sixty-five degrees, a little chilly for a massage!

I finished my massage, and walked my client out. As I came back in, the dude from the office in front of me held the door open.

I was a little shocked as he barely even returned greetings and had made disparaging remarks about massage to my partner, Tammi.

I said, "Oh, thank you, sir!" as I stepped through the opened door. He whipped around and growled, "You turned it up to—98 degrees in here, I *had* to open the door!"

I took a breath and said, "Oh, I'm sorry, it got too hot. I only put it on seventy-one."

"Maybe if you didn't work in shorts blah, blah, blah," he said. I tuned out after the attack on my attire. I ignored that last remark, in a very saint like fashion, I might add, and returned to my shop to clean up. As I walked out to my car, Mr. Wonderful is in the middle of telling his story to a lady from upstairs.

"Yeah, she had that heat turned up to ninety-eight degrees."

I interrupted, "Seventy-one. It was on sixty-five degrees, and I put it on seventy-one because my clients are just wearing a sheet, it has *nothing* to do with me wearing shorts!"

That silenced him. I just couldn't let him stand there and bald faced lie about me.

A few days later, another shop owner in the building told my partner, "Hey, I heard you had it out with Mr. Wonderful!" Word had gone through the building apparently. Don't tread on me!

I was so proud of myself for standing up to this guy. He was being a bully. I have spent my life defending others against bullying—even wrote a curriculum on antibullying once but have never defended me until the last few years.

Needless to say, I felt kinda good about myself. Yet . . . not. There was this odd little twitch when I thought about the whole thing.

Welp, the other day I went to the shop for an appointment. Mr. Wonderful was just walking in his office and closing the door behind him. Before I could stop myself, my hand was knocking on his door.

I screamed to myself, "WHAT ARE YOU DOING?" and tried desperately to command my hand to stop.

He turned back and pulled open the door, shocked and perhaps even a little apprehensive. I am pretty threatening with my ninja skills and all.

Something took over my body. Aliens. Elvis. Whitney Houston maybe—was that you Whitney? My lips opened and this strange voice said,

"Listen, I just really want to apologize for the other day. It obviously got much warmer in your office than ours. I'm sorry I blew you out and I'll figure out something different."

His jaw dropped for a brief moment before he looked down and began shuffling imaginary papers on his desk, muttering, "Oh no, no big deal, that's fine."

I told him to have a great day as I left. I promptly went out and slammed my head in the car door repeatedly, silently screaming, "You idiot! He had it coming! He lied! He was hateful and mean! I was right, he was wrong!"

I mean, that's all that mattered, was that I was *right*, right?
Wrong.

It felt good to draw a boundary with a bully, don't misunderstand me. God doesn't call us to be doormats.

He does, however, call us to be peacemakers. Even says we will be blessed for being one.

"Blessed are the peacemakers . . ."

"Seek peace and pursue it . . ."

"A soft answer turns away wrath . . ."

Those scriptures are *truth*. I spent so many years more worried about my pride and my "rightness" that I impaired relationships. When we hang on to an offense, it rolls around in our soul and body, making us ill.

Seek peace. Use soft answers when someone is being a jerk face. Humble yourself . . . for that is where he dwells.

Now, I and Mr. Wonderful have a new fledgling professional relationship. We say hello to each other now, with a smile, born of a shared moment of making it through a relational fire together.

So—let the Holy Spirit take over your speech, he has so much more grace. And what a difference grace makes. It's amazing!

Chapter 60

It was my very first week of hospice training. I had walked through a lot of death, including the death of my father, but nothing *really* prepares you for hospice work.

As Chaplain Carolyn Clark Heltzel was training me and taking me around to visit patients, I met a little lady I would never forget. She was at the end of the hallway in a room by herself in the nursing home. As we entered Mrs. Marie's room, the sight before me made me catch my breath.

In the bed was a tiny little lady, with her head bent almost to her chest, her feet askew, her hands clenched permanently into fists, and drawn to her chest. To introduce myself and visit with her, I had to lean over the bed and twist in order to look into her eyes.

Those eyes. Twinkling blue eyes. As I visited with her, leaning over the bed, I began to get the twinge of a headache. I've been in a lot of car wrecks and have always suffered from migraines and a stiff, sore neck. I was thinking how my head was beginning to hurt from twisting my neck, and feared a migraine coming on.

We wrapped up the visit, and after prayer, Mrs. Marie began to softly whisper in a sing-song voice, "When I wake up in the morning, and when I lay my head to rest, I am blessed, I am blessed."

Wow! Every bit of physical discomfort I had felt, vanished beneath the weight of the words just spoken aloud. I was whining about a little neck ache, and this beautiful woman with a broken body is telling me how blessed she is? Nobody but the Holy Spirit can teach those types of lessons in humility, pain, and suffering.

That day I saw grace in the midst of pain; strength in the midst of weakness; and a determination to praise in the midst of the storm.

Can we *all* be as brave as my little Mrs. Marie? Oh, she is no longer confined to that bed by the way.

But then—*she never was.*

Chapter 61

Mrs. P was a neat little lady. I would have to make sure I had plenty of time for my visits with her as we had amazing, rambling conversations.

She was in a nursing home as she could no longer care for herself. She had a great relationship with her children and grandchildren.

The problem was, she was in a lot of pain and discomfort. No matter what combination of medications that we used, she often suffered from nausea, vomiting, and just generalized pain.

Every visit, her prayer request was that Jesus would take her "home." During this time, she sold her home, and distributed her items accordingly among her family. She put everything "in order" and was "ready to go,"

Yet—she lived. She would cry and say that she didn't know why the Lord wouldn't just "take her." We would pray, and I would always encourage her to pray like Jesus in the garden, asking the father to "take this cup, but nevertheless, *thy will* be done."

This went on for months and months. Then, one day before we prayed, I said, "Well, I know what your request is."

She looked at me with a peace I had not yet seen, and said, "No, Barbie, I don't want to pray that anymore. Now, I just want what Jesus wants."

Wow. She had been a woman of faith for over seventy years, yet still struggled. God showed me then and there that no matter how old we are, or how long we have walked in faith, it is a life-long surrendering to his will and crucifying our own.

Not long after, Mrs. P went "home." Our battles will be shortened the sooner that we get to the place of "just wanting what Jesus wants."

I begged God for my will to be done, and in his loving faithfulness, he said, "NO." When I laid it down, and said, "I just want what *you* want." He gave me something so much more precious and beautiful than I even knew to ask for!

Today—just "want what Jesus wants." You'll be amazed at what is waiting on the other side.

Chapter 62

It started out like every other day, too early. My son Nick wasn't quite three, Jake not quite two. Josh would join us by that time the next year.

I worked for the Department of Veteran Affairs in the Vocational Rehabilitation and Counseling (VR&C) Office. As part of my job duties, I got to travel to our out based locations and do training occasionally.

One of our other main offices was in Oklahoma City in the Alfred P. Murrah building. Our staff there and the other locations were really more like one big family. After I had my boys, my friend Dianne would talk about a young mother with two young sons that she saw every morning as the mother dropped them off at the daycare in the federal building. She said it always made her think of me, toting around two toddlers.

Well, the morning coffee drinkers were on their second pot, people were taking their first break of the morning, smokers were smoking . . . when the call came. One of our OKC staff members called and in shock. He said the building had just blown up. He had run for blocks after getting out, and called into our office. I don't remember how we heard, but at first they suspected a gas leak was to blame. The horrible truth would be revealed along with threats against our building as well.

We were desperate to account for all of our VA staff. As news trickled in, one by one they were accounted for, except Dianne. We were heartsick and confused.

Richard Merritt and I got together and prayed, all those years ago, at his desk. I don't recall how we finally got word, but Dianne was eventually located in one of the hospitals.

Her story was one of so many miraculous survivor testimonies. She was on her way downstairs to a meeting, when another one of our staff members called her, running late (saving his life and hers that day). He asked Dianne to look something up on a veteran for him. When she finished, she realized she would be late to the 9:00 a.m. meeting, so she ran down the stairwell instead of waiting on the elevator. Just as she reached the bottom floor and pushed open the door, the bomb exploded. She was thrown back and her wrist shattered.

Every person she was going to meet with had been killed in the blast. She later said she thought she had triggered the explosion because it happened the instant she pushed the door open. Many others had similar stories of doing something at that moment and thinking they had triggered something.

The young mother with the two sons would be on the news in the coming days as she laid both of her children to rest.

Our hearts were broken and some part of innocence died as evil took the stage for a brief moment. It was brief because Oklahomans came together in prayer, love, kindness, and support.

Dianne didn't trigger the bomb that day. However, nineteen years later, in a little country church, Richard Merritt would recall that day in prayer together, and how that he heard the Holy Spirit when I prayed. As we work side by side in ministry now, I would say that God triggered *many* amazing things that day as he overcame evil with good as people poured out his love and stories of the miraculous abounded.

May the families of the 168 victims and the 680 injured survivors of that day, April 19, 1995, be comforted beyond measure. That day drove us to our knees, may the remembrance of it keep us there.

Chapter 63

The air was filled with anxiety as holiday shoppers pushed past one another, looking for sales, eyes shifting about greedily.

There were so many people, that even she did not stand out. She was covered head to toe in the clothing her religion demands. Except for warm, brown eyes peeking out, all that you saw were folds and folds of black fabric.

She was trying on different bracelets, each filled with shiny stones. A young girl, presumably her daughter, walked up and they chattered a moment in a language from far away.

She was asking her daughter's opinion as my eyes met hers. I told her they were both beautiful on her, she should get both. I held up two fingers as I said this, and she laughed aloud.

I found myself reflecting on what it would be like to live a life covered, head to toe, hidden beneath layers and layers.

Then I realized that I had lived just like this woman. My body wasn't covered in that way, but my heart was.

Layers upon layers, hidden beneath my religion, my sarcasm, my self-righteousness.

I thanked God for peeling back those layers of pride and pain, making me transparent.

My attention shifted back to the cloaked figure in front of me.

Though separated by our culture, our religion, and our language, we found a common ground in admiring a shiny bracelet.

As we smiled at one another, two women worlds apart, we transcended all of it and shared a moment of sisterhood.

And I shall stay ever watchful to never again cover myself or my heart with anything but the love of Christ, and always ready to encourage a sister—especially when it involves something shiny.

Chapter 64

I have never been into NASCAR. Maybe it's the ADHD that prevents me from watching people drive in circles, on purpose, for hours.

Yet here I was, my very first weekend in New York, working at a NASCAR race at Watkins Glenn Speedway. The bestie found the job on Craigslist on our way to New York.

We were going to serve in the VIP tent for the race.

Now, we all moved to New York without anything—no money, no jobs, no house. The only thing that we had was our faith and each other.

We arrived at the track while it was still dark outside. We were given our assignments as we all shivered in the early morning mist that engulfed us.

The VIP tent was set up right by the Starting/Finish Line. As I surveyed how close I was, I made a mental note of which way to run if a car flipped my way!

I really can't describe the energy and excitement that coursed through my veins as I heard "Gentlemen, start your engines," the vibration and sound of all those cars was electrifying!

You could hear tires squeal as they grabbed the pavement, feel the heat from the powerful engines, and smell competition and fuel in the air.

It was one of the most exciting things I have ever witnessed.

See, that's the difference—I could say I'm not a NASCAR fan, but it wasn't a fair statement because I had not yet *experienced* NASCAR.

It was the same thing with my life of faith. I was an onlooker—I told everyone else about God's love and forgiveness, but I had not experienced it yet in my own life. I was driving in circles.

Experience makes all the difference. If you have not wept with the realization of God's love, forgiveness, grace, and mercy—for *you*—then you, too, may be an onlooker to a life of faith.

When those engines started in New York, my engine started. I resolved to stop looking back at the train wreck that was my life, and look forward to being back in the race.

I would go to another NASCAR race, any day. And I will walk this life with passion and a running engine *every* day.

Gentlemen and women, start your engines!

Chapter 65

Niagara Falls is something I have wanted to see most of my life. I think from the first time I read of it, in fifth grade social studies, I wanted to go.

When I knew that I was moving back to Oklahoma, the *one* thing I didn't want to leave New York without *experiencing* was Niagara Falls. So Sean Thomas took me. Me, the bestie, and my favorite seven-year-old.

There are a few different falls. One of them moves over six hundred thousand gallons of water per second! To actually be there, to hear the roar of the water, feel the immensity and power . . . to have the spray on my face—*unbelievable!*

I mean, I have read about it. I have seen pictures and movies. But there is *nothing* that compares to experiencing it for myself.

It is the same with the love, grace, and mercy of God. I have devoted most of my broken life to sharing those attributes of God with hurting people. All the while, though, I had not yet truly experienced it for myself. I didn't even know . . .

Until—I could do nothing else but seek *him*. What I found was an immense power and the deafening roar of his love. I stood a broken woman as his grace splashed upon my face, renewing me. I wondered at how I had even "run dry" when all of this living water was available and abundant!

I will never "see" Niagara Falls the same way because I have experienced and been a part of it, even if for a brief moment in time.

It is the same with God's love. I still feel the splash in my soul, the moving of six hundred thousand gallons of his grace pouring over me every second.

May you all experience the splash today!

Chapter 66

As I travelled, I chatted with my nephew on my cell phone. I was on my way to see my two sons compete in the State Speech and Debate competition at the University of Oklahoma (OU).

The rain began to come down in sheets as I realized that I had missed my exit. I told my nephew goodbye so I could focus on driving in the storm. Anyone who knows me very well knows that I often take the "scenic route" to my destination. Not on purpose, mind you, it just keeps happening.

After turning around a billion miles down the road, I exited the freeway to head into Norman.

The storm had passed and it was eerily still as I entered the town. The further I drove, the more confused I became. Where was everyone? Why were there trees broken everywhere?

By the time I neared the campus, people were just beginning to trickle outside, surveying the damage.

The road to the campus was blocked with emergency vehicles as a power line dangled from the pole snapped in half above it.

I kept trying to call my boys, but they didn't answer.

I turned around and went to check in to the hotel I was staying at. As I checked in, I said "Wow, what a storm!"

The guy said, "Actually, a tornado just went through here twenty minutes ago!"

I was stunned.

I checked into my room and finally got word that my boys were safe in the basement at OU.

Had I not "accidentally" missed my exit, I would have been driving at the same time and on the same path as that tornado.

What seemed like a wrong turn and a waste of time may actually have saved my life.

And so it is with the "wrong turns" we make in life. We can berate ourselves for the time we have wasted, or we can believe that the path we took spared us from an even worse fate.

As I took the "wrong path," my sons were safe and secure because God is just that *big* and just that *good*.

So—thank God for missed turns, wrong turns, and U-turns—knowing that he works it *all* together for our good.

Chapter 67

I remember I was about six years old as I didn't yet know how to swim. My family was at the lake, and my dad was out in the water, working on our boat.

Well, I decided to go see him.

I walked out there in the water, and by the time I reached him, my face was barely above water, with my head tilted back to breath. My mom was yelling "Smitty, get Barbie!" My dad looked at me and said, "You got yourself out here, you get yourself back." I turned my little trash can around and went back to the safety and surety of the shore.

That's so been the story of my life. Wading out in places I didn't belong . . . almost over my head . . . My heavenly dad was with me, and in me, but I still heard him whisper, "You got yourself out here, you get yourself back." And step by step, day by day, I walk out of the deep water I myself walked into in the first place.

And I thank my father for the training.

Chapter 68

I couldn't believe this was my life.

My dad had just passed away, and I was no longer with head start. Hospice wasn't even a thought yet, as I searched for employment. A friend from church offered me a job, and I couldn't refuse it.

I delivered and set up home medical equipment for home health and hospice patients. We drivers also had the honor of cleaning said equipment when it returned.

Wheelchairs, bedside commodes, beds, mattresses—all came back in a much "different" state than we sent them in. It was humbling to say the least. I was certain I was called to preach, so I really didn't understand this twist in my story.

One day, I was feeling particularly hopeless and confused. However, I put on my "happy face" and went out to deliver equipment.

I was in Okmulgee in a little Indian woman's home setting up her oxygen. I explained everything to her as I knelt there in her tiny living room.

After I finished with the tanks, she said, "You are a Christian, aren't you?" A little shocked, I replied that I indeed was.

She said, "The love of God shines through you. You don't understand right now, but you are right where you are supposed to be."

I knelt there, riveted to the floor by her words and her penetrating stare as she spoke them.

The whole exchange lasted but a moment, but it was such a *holy* moment. It seemed all the air had been sucked from the room as her words hung there in the deafening silence.

Finally, with my eyes filled with tears, I got off my knees, and hugged her tiny frame. I thanked her the best I could, but we both knew it was a gift from above.

I went there to deliver oxygen to a dying woman.

Turns out, she delivered oxygen to the woman dying in me.

Chapter 69

I first met her when she walked into the hospital room with Mom, Dad, and me. We had no idea what hospice was and had been given the devastating news that treatment was no longer an option for my dad's lung cancer.

She came in like a ray of light in our darkness. She kindly explained hospice to us and completed all of the admission paperwork.

The next one-and-a-half years (a story and miracle in itself), she visited my dad monthly or more. She always cracked us up!

Two years had gone by since my dad crossed over, and I found myself now working side by side with her. Day after day, and death after death together.

I left hospice a few years later, and within a week or so of my leaving, she was diagnosed with cancer, and there was nothing they could do.

It shocked and devastated everyone.

She had loved and lost several times in her life. She had recently been in a new relationship, taking trips and enjoying life with this man.

I visited her several times in the hospital. During my last conversation with her, she said, "Barbie, I asked God to let me fall in love and be loved one last time before I died."

Her new boyfriend was in and out of the picture, and all that loved her had some anger that he felt he couldn't handle this journey with her.

Just a few days after our conversation, she was sent home to die. The next evening, I got the call that she was passing, and nonresponsive.

I had already said my "goodbye for now" and was no longer a part of the hospice team yet felt led to go. So I did.

Many surrounded her, and her little house was full. I was there, still dressed in camo as I had been hunting and just killed a deer when I got the call.

I went into her little kitchen, and there, alone, sat her boyfriend. I went in and sat with him in the heavy silence.

I began to feel led to tell him what she had said about loving and being loved one more time. I argued as that was a private conversation between she and I.

"Tell him." Finally, I obeyed and shared that with him. His eyes filled with tears, and right then, someone came and got him and asked him to come in there with her.

I sat there, alone in grief and wondering again why I was there.

Just a moment or two went by, and she passed from this life.

A week or so later, I told the story about talking to him to one of our mutual best friends. She looked at me and told me a story that gave me goose bumps to my toes and made me so thankful for that voice.

She said that her boyfriend walked into that room, bent down, and told her that he loved her—then she passed.

God had given her what she asked. And God gave me yet another glimpse of his love and power and divine direction.

Tell someone today that you love them. They may just be dying to hear it.

Chapter 70

Soooo . . . I've *never* actually packed a Penske moving truck. It is quite the feeling of accomplishment! Stacking, evaluating, and placing boxes just so to get the *most* use of the space. It was some really tight squeezes. Layer, after layer, after layer.

Now, it's time to unpack that same truck.

I'm really the best one to get up in there and take all those things back out of that truck. I'm the one that put them in there, so I remember and just "know" how to take them back out without everything crashing down around my ears!

And it's layer, by layer, by layer.

Here's the thing. We spend our early years and adulthood "packing." Packing pain, joy, experiences, heartache. We have layers and layers.

Regardless of what "choices" we have made, God is sovereign over it all.

I kept trying to "unpack my truck," change myself, be a "better Christian" strip off the layers.

The thing is, there is only *one* who truly knew how things were "put" into me, so he is the best one to take them back out! Layer, after layer, after layer.

Don't try to fix your life, or unpack your junk. Turn to the one that knows how those things got in you in the first place, and let him pull them back out. He's much more gentle than I ever knew.

He's a master unpacker.

Chapter 71

Every year, I swear it will be different. Yet here I am again. I have not bought one Christmas present yet. Not one. I am one of those last minute idiots out there shocked at all the other last minute idiots!

I do some of my best work under pressure—always have. That's what I tell myself when "myself" starts berating me for being a procrastinating bum.

Year after year, frenzied shopping and all night wrapping sessions, sipping cocoa, and trying not to cut any of my fingers off with sharp things.

I don't recall what I had done with the stockings from the year before, but here I was—stockingless.

Three boys, and five adults (I had company) needed something to hang from the chimney with care.

I found myself shopping, at the last minute, with a bunch of idiots.

My quest took me from store to store without a stocking in sight. I had already bought the "stuffers" so it was life or death to find some dadgum stockings!

I was about to head back home in defeat, when I saw a picture in my head. Giggling with the craziness of it, I headed back into the frenzy for my items.

After wrapping presents into the wee hours of the morning, I finally lay my head to rest.

Christmas morning dawned upon my household, and we all began to gather in the family room.

There, hung by the chimney with care, were the eight pot holders that I used for stockings!

They had loopy thingies to hang, they were nice Christmas prints . . . they held stuff!

Turns out, I didn't wreck Christmas with my idiotic procrastination, instead, a last-minute inspiration gave us all a chuckle and a memory.

And if Christmas isn't about laughing with friends and family, making memories, then I think we don't truly understand the spirit of Christmas.

We can put so much pressure on ourselves this time of year. I say to myself and to you, take a deep breath, exhale *slowlyyyyy*. It all works out, so laugh, smile . . . and know that a pot holder works as a Christmas stocking in a pinch.

If you are one of those idiots out there at the last minute, I'll see you there!

Chapter 72

My eyes widened as I pulled up into the driveway. Roman columns graced the front of the home, and various large statues were placed throughout the immaculately cared for lawn. A vine covered archway invited you to walk under it and discover what lay beyond.

I double-checked my paperwork, making sure that I was indeed in the right place. I was.

This magnificent home was located in a small town, and seemed almost out of place amidst the farm houses and brick homes surrounding it.

I was there to meet my newest hospice admit, a young man in his early forties. This was his mother's home as she was caring for him as he walked the journey out of this world and into the next one.

The woman that greeted me at the door was a weary soul. Her perfectly coifed hair and manicured nails were in sharp contrast to her puffy eyes and the tight line of her mouth, now attempting a smile.

The home was as grand inside as it was out. I walked upon the marble floors admiring the works of art upon the walls. We sat on the oversized furniture as we began to visit.

My patient, the woman's son, lay on the couch, somewhere between this world and the other, unconscious.

At first, she was very cautious and guarded with her story as I was a complete stranger. Gradually, her story began to spill from her lips as the pain propelled it.

She had three sons, like me. One son lived nearby, one was in prison, and one lay dying on her couch from the lifelong effects of drugs and alcohol.

She and her husband accumulated their wealth by owning and operating a business for over thirty years. Her husband finally made the decision to retire as his life had been consumed by his work. They made plans to take all those trips they never took, because there just wasn't "time."

They sold their business, and a week or so before he retired, he was killed in a car wreck.

This huge home was filled with possessions, yet empty of life and starved for love. The heart broken wife and mother before me was inconsolable with mere words.

As she shared her pain, tears ran down both of our cheeks.

I had no words of comfort; I could only listen with growing sorrow and a realization that the road ahead of her was not going to be any easier than the road behind her, at least not for a while.

She was filled with regret of what was and what would never be. Nothing prepares a mother to care for her dying child.

I don't yet know the end of this family's story, so I cannot share a happy ending with you here. I just know that we all get one.

What I do hope to share is what this families pain taught me. I have made a conscious decision to live, here, now. She and her husband missed life, working and waiting for retirement to live it.

Don't wait to travel or do that thing you've always wanted to do. Hold your sons and your daughters often, and very close to your heart as you never know where life may take them later.

It doesn't matter if you live in a mansion, yet don't live life within it's walls. Possessions cannot bring peace. We spend our health getting wealth, then our wealth trying to regain our health.

Take walks. Hold hands with the one you love. Laugh with your babies. Chase beautiful sunsets and smell wild flowers. Live life now.

After all, now is all that is promised.

Chapter 73

The man sitting across from me was completely devastated. His entire life had changed in a matter of hours. One minute, he was at a "Relay for Life" cancer event, the next, a cold hospital waiting room.

His beautiful wife was the chairperson for the event, and had just been interviewed there by the news. She suddenly got a terrible migraine, was taken to the hospital, life-flighted, and was gone by 7:00 a.m. the next morning. She left behind an eleven-year-old son, five-year-old daughter, and this broken man in front of me.

When the funeral home called me to do the funeral, they said that all the other ministers they called refused to do it because the husband didn't want a "sermon" at his wife's funeral.

As he sat before me, he told me of being wounded in a church. He loved Christ. His wife loved Christ. All he wanted to do though was get the service *over* with so he could as he said, "Just take my wife home (her ashes)."

We met for coffee as he poured out his heart, slowly, after gaining enough trust to do so. There was a question of fault with a medicine administered to his wife that made her brain swell so much that it popped her brain stem. He was enraged as well as bewildered.

I outlined the service, and asked permission to pray and read scripture. He was good with that.

The day of the funeral came, and even though I arrived early, the parking lot was overflowing. There were hundreds of people there as this woman loved and touched so many in her community.

I went in to the family, and met this beautiful five-year-old angel and eleven-year-old boy thrust into adulthood through death. I brought them both stuffed animals, a last minute inspiration.

I felt like I met Cindy through her daughter! This little girl was so vibrant and overflowing with love and life! My heart was in my throat as I surveyed the family and thought of the task before me.

As I began the service, and the family walked in, you could feel the weight of tragedy and grief among the masses.

The beautiful little girl began to call out greetings to those in the crowd she knew! "Hi, Mrs. So-and-So!" "Hi, Mrs. So and So!" and, slowly, giggles began to erupt as the pall of grief was broken by life and love in a little girl; a carbon copy of her mother.

As the video of "Cindy's" life played on the screen, her daughter waved at her throughout and said "hi mommy!"

I almost lost it completely at that point. I thought of her daughters first menstrual cycle, her first crush, her first date, her first prom, her wedding . . . all of the things a girl needs a mother for. The holy spirit brought me a knowing that he had *all* that under control.

Somehow, I got up and finished. We showed the news reel, taken hours before her death, at the Relay for Life Event.

We are truly all in this relay together, and our life is our message! I honored God in Cindy's life that day, and it was easy because she lived by *love*.

A sermon was preached that day. Other ministers missed an enormous blessing because of dogmatic traditions.

Why would we not take any and every opportunity to minister to the wounded and brokenhearted?

That day, hundreds of people were ministered to without one single "sermon." It just took the unconditional love and hope of a five-year-old little girl.

Cherish those around you, and make sure as you go through your days you call out in love to those around you in love and enthusiasm, "Hi, Mrs. So and So!"

Chapter 74

Laura was a lady that did my payroll for my daycare in Nevada. After I sold my business, I went to work with her for a couple months until I moved back to Oklahoma.

Our relationship was purely business—until I began waking up in the middle of the night with her face before me. I had learned that I was to pray for the person when that happened. I didn't know what, or why, but trusted God with that.

One morning, in the shower, (hey, some of my greatest conversations with God happen there—don't judge me!) her face came before me again, and I clearly heard in my spirit.

"Tell her to remember me."

What? What does that even mean? No way, she'll think I'm a freak! On and on with all the reasons I couldn't and wouldn't—and just that insistent, gentle voice that spoke the world into being—"Remember Me."

I got to the office, and Vicki walked out and said, "Hey, I want to take you to lunch today."

Ughhhh! "Of course you do," I thought. For a couple of hours, I tried to plan how to deliver the message without looking like an idiot or freaking her out!

We sat down for lunch, and I began sharing "my story." Laura looked at me, expressionless. I couldn't read her at all! As I blabbed on and on, all I heard was "Remember Me."

We finished up lunch, and headed back to the office. I was almost physically ill. Just before we walked back in, I touched her arm and said,

"Laura—I've been praying for you at night—I mean, not that you need prayer or anything (I didn't want to offend her after all!), and this morning, God told me to tell you "Remember Me."

I'll never forget that moment. She began to cry—actually, weep. I held her for what seemed an eternity before she straightened herself and said, "Thank you, Barbie."

We walked back in and never spoke of it again. But she began to send me inspirational e-mails and we had a new bond formed in heaven.

I never knew what that meant to her, but she did. God showed me the power of obedience and trust in him.

A couple of years ago, I was in a very, very dark place. God felt far away. One day, in the midst of crying out to him, I heard "Remember Me." He took me back to that hot day in Nevada, and the power of his words to free a woman's soul.

Not—remember your own pain and heartache, your own suffering—but Remember Me in your pain and suffering.

Once again, God showed me that the words we give to others in love are often the keys to our own chains and shackles.

Today, remember *him*. He that has captured your every tear, and has the very hairs of your head numbered.

You'll never be the same.

Chapter 75

I was preparing to do a funeral (common theme in my life, I know), and needed a suit. Funds were low, so I went to a little resale boutique that had just opened. I found just the one! It was a beautiful caramel color, and fit me like it was made for me. No one would ever guess I got this little bargain for less than $30!

I had not met the woman I was doing the funeral for. I met with her husband and family, and listened to their stories to get a sense of her. When I went home, I went in prayer as always. I told God that I didn't know this woman, but he did. I asked him for the message, a personal one, the one the family needed and the one that would honor him and her life.

Let me tell you . . . God gave me a message in forty-five seconds. I had gone to see a movie; and he gave me a metaphor of the movie, the woman's life, and his plans and purposes for us. It was truly the best message I had ever heard!

The next morning I put on my "new" suit, and went to preach and encourage. There were hundreds of people there. I was a little nervous as I had never delivered this message before. I began to preach, and it was going quite well. I noticed a pastor in the crowd, and every time I happened to look his way, he nodded at me. I mean I was getting after it—talking with my hands like I always do, looking like I was landing a 747! The pastor's kind gaze and nod helped me know I wasn't drifting into heresy too much. I was truly in awe of the message the Holy Spirit gave me. At the end of the funeral, as people passed by, they remarked about the message.

As the pastor approached, I just knew he was going to say that the message changed his life forever or ask me to take over his congregation, or be the pope . . . or something like that.

As he walked up, he leaned in closely and whispered . . . "You have a yellow tag hanging under your arm."

Throughout that whole message, I had a big yellow resale tag hanging underneath my arm! Man, oh, man—just when you think you're cool.

Chapter 76

When I was a little girl, one of the things I loved to do was go fishing with my mom and dad. Well, I loved or I hated it, depending on if the fish were biting. My parents would throw their lines out, patiently waiting decades for a catfish to swim by.

Me, I fished for crappie. Why? Because I got to cast over and over. I didn't have the patience to just . . . sit. I had to always be doing something.

One of the places we fished was the banks of the Arkansas River. My dad had an old green pickup truck we would drive. It had three gears and a smoker's cough. We would bounce along the dirt road with deep ruts in it, lined with trees on each side and the smell of the river permeating the air.

One of the highlights of the trip would be when my dad would put me on his lap and let me "drive" down that dirt road on the way home. That old truck would bounce from rut to rut as my little hands tried to keep it between them. I always had an uncanny ability to head toward the biggest tree.

Just when it seemed disaster was imminent, my dad's big hands would cover mine on the steering wheel as he took control of the vehicle and kept not just me, but all of us, from harm.

My dad taught me the value of just sitting—in hope and expectation. There is a time to cease from doing.

And—

Every time that I have steered my life into disaster, or been bounced from one painful rut to another, God's big hands covered mine as he rescued me from disaster and steered me into his peace.

On my own, I have a tendency to steer toward the ruts and the trees.

I know my daddy has me on his lap and just lets me "think" I'm in charge as we journey together down this old dirt road home.

But I still keep both hands on the wheel.

Chapter 77

I received a call that one of my patients had passed. We were unable to contact his wife of sixty-three years, so I was to go to their home while the social worker stayed at the nursing home. They were the neatest little Indian couple. I silently hoped she would go to the nursing home first so that I did not have to be the one to tell her.

Her granddaughter answered the door and let me in. As I sat on the couch, preparing to tell her about her grandfather, my eyes fell upon a very disturbing sight.

On the couch lay their grandson, looking to be in his midtwenties. He had Down syndrome as well as some type of neuromuscular disease.

That's not what was disturbing. What made me freeze in my track was that his hands were tied together with a rope. He lay there, speaking unintelligibly, and putting his hands behind his head repeatedly, kicking his legs.

I had come to give "bad news," and now I was faced with a clear case of abuse to report. As I struggled for words, I told his sister that there are medical "soft restraints" that could be purchased for use if restraint is necessary. They are much more "civilized" than a rope though I didn't say that.

She said that they had tried them all, but he harmed himself even more with those, pulling his hair out by the handfuls, and punching himself. She explained that he seemed more content with the rope and didn't harm himself this way.

I was taken aback, again. I heard the verse "I will heal and *bind up* the wounded and brokenhearted." This girl clearly loved her brother, and he seemed so content, cooing on the couch. I saw no marks on his body, no hair missing from his head.

The grandmother came home, and I delivered the news that Mr. C had passed. In typical Indian fashion, she didn't say much, just thanked me for being there and letting her know. As I drove away, the verse came to me again—"I will heal and *bind* up (tie, fasten) the wounded and brokenhearted."

God showed me the chains of my own life and how even though they had felt like bondage to me at the time, he was keeping me from harming myself *even* more. He bound me for my sake.

I realized that that young man was much freer than I was at that time. God was lovingly caring for him as he cared for me—even though at first glance it seemed barbaric.

Trust God. He knows when to bind us and when to loose us. Look beyond what you see with your natural eyes, and you will find the loving hand of a father, that is tending to your every hurt.

Even if he has to use a rope to do it.

Chapter 78

The sun was shining brightly with a gentle breeze blowing. The neighborhood looked like countless other neighborhoods with duplexes and craftsman style bungalows.

As she ate her SpaghettiOs, the little girl watched the scene unfolding before her, almost impassively. She was just a few years old as she watched her father bash her mother's head into the driveway repeatedly.

Her mother's screams for help went unmet. There was no neighborhood hero coming to her rescue. Domestic violence was so normal that the child never left the bench she sat upon.

Almost forty years and two lifetimes later, that scene replayed over and over in the girl's mind. Now, it was she that cowered beneath the anger and violence of another. The screams were now her screams as she found herself fighting for her life as her mother had before her.

The girl was devastated and bewildered at the life of violence and abuse she had willingly participated in. When did it become okay to have another person choke you and punch you and then convince you that you deserved it?

As the scene from those early years flashed more and more, the numbness began to wear off. Soon, the scene had sound instead of just the picture that had replayed over and over. She began to not only hear her mother's cries for help, but she began to feel them.

No one came to her mother's rescue. Her mom had to make a choice and walk out of that life while she still had a life. Now, the girl faced the same decision as each "episode" had become more dangerous.

Our first few years are the most important in our development. We learn love, empathy, and security among a million other things. The girl went back to those first few years and realized why abuse felt so normal. Until she faced that, her cries for help went unmet too.

It was a battle to change the way she thought, but she couldn't endure the pain of making the same mistake over and over.

After praying for and receiving divine strength, the girl came to her own rescue as her mother had to a lifetime before. She answered her own cries for help so that she could finally get off that bench she had been on all those years.

The sun shone brightly as she wiped the spaghetti sauce off of her chin and stood up to rescue herself.

Sometimes, you have to be your own hero.

Chapter 79

Two months ago today, I had my head shaved for St. Baldrick's—an amazing organization dedicated to finding the cure for childhood cancer.

Let me be clear—I had *zero* intention of doing so! The bestie and my fave seven-year-old came home from school, completely moved by the story of St. Baldrick's. The seven-year-old called me to the table for a family meeting and informed me that we were *all* participating! I said, "No way, but thank you!"

Those that know me, know how I feel about cancer. My mother is a breast cancer survivor, my father passed in 2005 from lung cancer, a very close friend just battled breast cancer, and as a hospice chaplain, I had witnessed over and over the devastation of cancer.

My reasoning was that I would have done it "back then" for my loved ones. As the event grew closer, I talked with Tammi about her shaving her head. I told her that I was afraid I would have just made an "emotional" decision, then have to "live with it."

Side note: During this time, I set my alarm to wake me up with the song "Eye of the Tiger." This is important, so remember it!

The night of the event finally came. Before we left (I was just going to be the photographer), I called Tammi into my room. I gave her implicit instructions to *not* let me get carried away there and shave my head!

Tammi and her hubby were the first group on stage. As her hair came off, and I filmed, I began to cry. The faces of my parents, my friend Shannon Cowden, and countless patients and families passed through my mind and soul. I cried and cried as Tammi began to glow from the inside out. After she was done, through my tears, I told her I thought I wanted to do it too.

I left with James to run home for a minute to clear my head! I went into my room and looked at my hair. I tried to imagine myself bald. As I battled, the *only* reason I could not imagine doing this was . . . *pride*. Something I am dedicated to dying to.

I got back to the event, and was *mostly* committed. As Tammi looked in my eyes and I went back and forth, "Eye of the Tiger" began to play!

Then, I knew. I knew I wasn't just jumping on the bandwagon. I knew I wasn't caught up in emotion. I knew that I knew! This was my wake-up call!

As the hair came off, I felt such an incredible peace and my loved ones battles became even more personal in *that* moment. I felt part of something so much bigger. I felt pride fall to the floor with my six-teen-plus inches of hair. If it was in my *hair* that I had pride—then take it all off! And—they did!

An amazing memory, all because of the heart and bravery of my best friend that did it *first*. I'll never be the same!

"It's the eye of the tiger, it's the thrill of the fight, rising up to the challenge of our rival!"

—with Tammi Benge Sawyer

Chapter 80

Steve was the cutest dog ever. He was born in my laundry room along with his seven brothers and sisters. Steve was named by my son Jake. He had a beautiful sandy blonde coat, and his fur was as soft as his sweet demeanor.

The only problem was we couldn't teach him to go up and down steps. We had to carry him as he was deathly afraid of them. This posed the biggest problem when letting Steve in and out to do his "business."

Though he was as dumb as the day was long, he stole our hearts from the beginning.

One night, after our home church, Steve didn't return from his potty break. I lived out in the forest and the closest neighbor at the time was a trek up through the dark woods. I could hear a dog barking and was convinced that Steve was on someone's porch, stuck, desperate for my help.

I put on my camouflage hunting clothes to go look for him. It was around eleven or so at night and very dark. I lit a Tiki torch and set off through the dark woods to rescue Steve.

I talked to one of my friends as I hiked, helping to allay my fears as my surroundings were like a Friday the thirteenth movie.

As I talked and headed toward the continual barking, I tripped and fell, igniting my hair for a brief moment with the Tiki torch.

Thankfully, I was dressed in camouflage, ensuring no one would find my body in the woods if I had a mishap.

I put out my hair, I got back up, and continued on my search and rescue mission. I finally arrived at the source of the barking and, alas, it wasn't my Steve.

Steve never came home, and though I continued searching, I never found him.

I am a mere human, yet I searched for my lost dog. Even though we are all a bit thick, and have crazy phobias and fears (like stairs), God searches out the darkest wildernesses for us.

My quest was unsuccessful, but God *never* is. I used a Tiki torch, but God illuminates the dark with his love and his spirit.

I didn't find my Steve, but God *always* finds his beloved.

No matter how dark your world may be, know there is one that does whatever it takes to bring you home.

No matter how dumb you are—I am living proof!

Chapter 81

Her bright, twinkling blue eyes threw me for a moment. There was so much mischief, just below the surface! Before me was my latest admit into hospice, a little lady at Broadway Manor. Nancy M. was one of the most interesting ladies I had ever met!

Her husband had passed away years before, and now she was preparing to meet him. They had travelled all over the world.

She loved to fly!

As we visited, she told me that she wanted to fly "one last time." One of my good friends, Danny Dunlap, was a pilot, and my brain started spinning. I visited with our hospice director and the nursing home director. With everyone on board, I called Danny.

We set up a date and met at Davis Field airport. The newspaper came out and took Nancy's picture and interviewed her.

You should have seen her face as we took off in that little plane! Death and disease stayed on the ground far below as we soared through the air. Danny let her "drive," and she just giggled like a schoolgirl.

That fabulous day was etched in my mind as I sat and prepared the message for Nancy's funeral. I loved her dearly, and her passion and zeal for life was unmatched.

The Muskogee Phoenix article said, "Woman flies one last time." But as I prepared to do her funeral, with a heavy heart, a little voice said, "Oh, I'm still flying!"

And someday, we will fly together again, Nancy M.!

—with Danny Dunlap

Chapter 82

"TWICE! You did it twice!" My mother's voice reverberated between my ears, insisting on being heard. She was referring to one of my favorite childhood stories, one that was a perfect illustration of how I continued to live my adult life.

I was just a toddler when I climbed upon the hood of the car, with a towel around my neck, and yelled, "Suuuuuperrrrmannnn" as I jumped off. My mom heard me, then heard my cries as the whole flying thing didn't quite pan out.

Mom came out, soothed me, and dusted me back off. She wasn't quite back in the house again when she heard, "Suuuuuperrrrmannnnn!"

Splat!

I guess I thought my technique must have been faulty on the first takeoff! I prolly did some intricate recalculating before my second attempt, but alas, the outcome was the same! Face down on the pavement.

Twice. As I looked at the broken pieces of my second attempt at marriage, I couldn't believe that I had failed not once, but twice. Two times I tied the towel of my own self will around my neck, as I climbed upon my pride and trusted in my own ability. I tried to save the world, yet here I found myself, facedown on the pavement a second time.

Despair and disillusionment met me as I came face to face with my own inability to save even myself, much less the world.

Twice. One failure could be explained away with a million excuses, but two? Had I really still been in pain from the first jump when I made the second? It was there, when I saw my own pride and arrogance that I stayed on my face and begged forgiveness.

For what? All of it. But for doing it my way. I took the towel off and surrendered the superpowers to the one they belong to. In laying down my will, the most beautiful grace and forgiveness began to heal my wounded heart and battered pride.

Then the most magical thing happened . . . Jesus dusted me off, just as my tough Irish mom had forty years before, and told me I didn't need a cape to begin with . . . I could fly all along! And now—I do.

I *fly*.

Above condemnation. Above reproach for making two jumps. I fly along on the wings of his grace, sailing on his mercy, reveling in his love.

Not once. Not twice. But forever.

Chapter 83

The scene was heartbreaking, like so many others in the Hospice world. Before me was a little lady in a hospital bed in her living room. Until just a month or two before, her husband's hospital bed was right beside her.

It was my only husband and wife on hospice at the same time. Neither of the patients was "religious" but allowed me to visit and pray with them. They had six children, losing both parents at almost the same time.

Mr. C passed, and I conducted his funeral. I continued my visits to his wife, who was not far behind him. One day, I received a call that Mrs. C was now nonresponsive, and the time was close for her to "cross over."

I arrived to find the house full of people, and our nurse. As I sat at her bedside, I kept feeling led to sing "Amazing Grace."

Well. Barbie does *not* sing. I mean, I do, but it sounds like a "coyote in a trash compactor" as my three boys say!

It wouldn't stop. "Amazing Grace."

No, God. This room is full of grieving people and you want me to bust out *this* voice?

So I did what I needed to do. I told the nurse that I thought God wanted her to sing "Amazing Grace"! Don't judge me.

She didn't go for it. She said she couldn't sing well either but agreed to help *me* sing.

We did. We began to sing that song, and Mrs. C began waking up! By the end of the song, she was fully alert again and speaking!

Her daughter started crying and said, "That's her *favorite* song!"

Obedience. Listen to that still small voice, no matter what kind of idiot you look like!

Chapter 84

When I was seven, I was climbing down from a tree house in barefoot. I was on an aluminum ladder, and I got my toes stuck in the braces and then fell a couple feet to the ground. The ladder chopped part of my middle toe and almost severed the toe next to it. Doctors tried to save both toes, but a few months later, my toe turned black and fell off in my shoe while I was playing.

I came home, distraught at losing a body part. My tough Irish mother was standing at the sink when I came in, freaked out that my toe fell off. Without batting an eyelash, my mom said, "Throw it in the trash." Then the trash was taken out and burned. You can't imagine the psychological damage this inflicted upon me!

Recounting the above trauma to my mother a few years ago, "How could you make me throw away *my own toe*?"

She replied, without batting an eyelash, "What did you want me to do? Put it under your pillow?"

Chapter 85

I was raised by my stepdad, who is really my dad. Along with this man came four bonus sisters. Cheryl, Cindy, Tina, and Shelly. They were all adults when I first met them. They lived in California and we lived in Oklahoma, making visits rare. I looked up to all of them for different reasons.

I do remember the first time I met Tina though. She was tall, gorgeous, and looked a lot like Dad.

I remember going to California when I was fourteen. We were all together when Tina came over in a cute little sports car. She always looked like a model to me—long legs, gorgeous everything, and a wit to match. We always had a great time exchanging sarcasm.

Tina endured tragedy in her life more than once. She withstood it, and she had a beautiful young daughter that was her world. When my dad was dying, we all came together and "step" was not a word we used or felt as we shared in our grief.

Tina and Dad had the same sense of humor. She was crazy about him, sitting in his chair to feel closer to him after he passed.

It was summer, and my dad had crossed over a couple years before. My sister Cindy was visiting from California, and Cheryl was here from Oklahoma City. Tina became ill suddenly (in Idaho, where she lived) and passed away. My sisters received the news, and it was so hard to believe.

Since we were all together, I suggested a memorial service here, just for us. I went one morning and aired up a couple dozen balloons (before I knew what they did to the environment), and we all gathered above the dam at the overlook. There was a picture of my dad and Tina—reminding us all where she was now—safe with her daddy and her heavenly daddy.

We shared funny family stories of her as we cried. Real stories because Tina was a real person. We listened to "I Can Only Imagine" as the tears streamed down, and we all stood silently with our memories.

We stood on that hillside with a gentle breeze blowing as we released those balloons and played Tina's favorite song, "Mustang Sally." It was so bittersweet to watch the balloons disappear from our sight, soaring above the very lake we used to all gather on and water ski growing up.

I drove out to the dam just yesterday and remembered that day and my beautiful bonus sisters.

Hug your family today. Call someone that you've been meaning to call.

I will always hear these words when I drive out by the dam and recall my beautiful sister,

"All you wanna do is ride around . . . ride, Sally, ride!"

Thankful today for my bonus sisters, and knowing that Tina is riding higher than us all, "Ride, Tina, Ride!"

Chapter 86

I scheduled a visit to a new hospice patient's home, but moments before I arrived, he expired. I met with the family for a bit, then went in with our nurse, Melinda, to help her prepare the body for the funeral home. She asked me to grab a clean T-shirt out of his drawer. I reached in and just grabbed the first one that I saw. We pulled it over his head, straightened it out, and read the words, "I Beat Cancer!"

Indeed.

Chapter 87

I stared down at my shoes, desperately trying to disappear. I knew that I was where I needed to be, yet still dumbfounded to find myself there.

I was at WISH—Women in Safe Homes. The year before, I had sat in that very chair discussing domestic violence and the young mother of four that I had just buried.

She was shot in her bathroom, point-blank, by the one that she loved and the one that claimed to love her.

I did a memorial service for her at the nursing home where she had worked. As I looked at all of the tear-stained faces, turned expectantly to me for words of comfort, I was struck by the Valentine decorations.

They seemed very out of place now as we memorialized a woman that loved the wrong man. I had a roll of red ribbon, and had the employees unravel it until everyone held a piece of that same red string, telling them that love and our love for her connect us all to one another.

Imagine my surprise to find that I was even more connected to her and her story than I knew.

As I sat there, the director of WISH told me that I was not loved, I was controlled, and that there *is* a difference. She told me that these things often end in death as though I had not seen that for myself.

Going to WISH was almost as hard as going to the police station. They took pictures of my bruises and my eyes that were filled with broken blood vessels from having my head crushed.

It was Valentine's Day, and I was filing a restraining order. As I walked through stores with stuffed animals and sentiments of love everywhere, the irony almost destroyed me.

Last year in New York, I worked on Valentine's Day. The sight of happy couples and families was bittersweet as I worked to remember that I was truly *loved*.

I had begged God for the love of one incapable of giving it. God very faithfully exchanged that broken idea of love and romanced me with his passionate pursuit of me.

I don't know how many times or how many years I will celebrate Valentine's Day and think of her . . .

The girl in a pool of her own blood in her bathroom and me in my own pool of pain—finally standing up for myself and desperately praying that my story wouldn't end like hers.

This year, I find myself in such a different place than I have ever known. I am in love and loved by the man of my dreams. I have less and less fear as I carve out the life I have always wanted.

A red ribbon connects us all—it is a ribbon of love and treasured memories.

Her ribbon intersected my ribbon and helped save my life. I pray my ribbon intersects others and brings them life as well.

His love is the greatest, and he never desires for his children to live in abuse. He died for us to have freedom, not fear.

As you see all of the hearts and roses, send up a prayer for those that are going through a silent hell. Keep your heart and your ears open to hear their cry.

Because someone heard mine, now I am going to die with memories instead of just dreams.

Chapter 88

It was the summer between my junior and senior year. I was embarking on a weeklong tour of the nation's capital, after winning an essay and speech competition.

Well. I was just a small town girl, living in a lonelyyyy world—wait, that's a *Journey* song. I digress. My point is, I graduated with thirty-one other people, and we were the largest class in years! I'm from Okay, Oklahoma. Population: Tiny! The 2011 census has it at just over six hundred people, so I was (and am) the epitome of "small town."

To say that I was intimidated is an understatement! The sights, sounds, smells—all so exciting, and I'm certain part of instilling such a love of diversity and travel. I got to see the Capital, Mount Vernon, Arlington, the monument . . . the wall. It was all so moving, and I felt like such a small speck in the cosmos.

Part of our week was getting to sit in on a either a senate or congressional hearing, memory fails me. I sat there feeling *very* small, surrounded by centuries of history and influence and power. A man in a suit came and sat down by me. As he surveyed my name tag, shaped like the state of Oklahoma with my name on it, he asked, "Oklahoma, huh? What part are you from?"

Well, people ten miles away haven't heard of Okay, Oklahoma, so I responded the way I had learned to through the years—"Oh, a small town outside of Muskogee."

He looked me in the eyes and said, "I was born and raised in Okay. Do you know Larry Drake? He was my best friend!"

Larry Drake was one of my dad's good friends, and I had gone to school with and was friends with his kids!

I could not tell you his name. I can only tell you—

It blew me away! We say "what a small world." I say, "What a big God! To reach down to a little girl in a big world and show her she was not alone . . . that the universe and our lives aren't just random notes of pain strung together, but beautiful harmonies intersecting and blending at appointed times, with the greatest maestro on earth orchestrating every note!

Chapter 89

She ordered a second glass of white wine after looking questioningly at her companion for permission. She looked to be in her sixties perhaps, and the man with her may have been her son.

I served them at Applebee's in New York. I came back out of the kitchen to find the lady staggering through the dining room. Her companion had gone to pull the car up, and she didn't know which way to go to get out.

I came alongside her, hooking my arm through hers. I was amazed that two glasses of wine were clearly too much for her to handle.

I wondered at what her life must be, to be inebriated this early in the afternoon. I was embarrassed for her as she staggered through the restaurant.

After I hooked my arm in hers and began walking her to the door, she muttered a few sentences that immediately changed my judgment.

She told me that she was recovering from her second brain tumor, and that most days she didn't know why God didn't just "take her."

I gripped her arm and told her that God had a plan and a purpose for her life as evidenced by the fact that she was still breathing.

She got misty eyed, hugged me tightly, and thanked me as I helped lift her into the waiting vehicle.

I judged her based only on what I saw and what few facts that I had. Every one that she staggered past did, I'm sure.

I was so humbled when she shared her story. Humbled and immediately convicted about my judgment.

Before you judge someone, hook your arm through theirs, lean in close, and listen to their story.

It just might stagger you.

Chapter 90

Her story is like so many of our stories . . . she really didn't know where she belonged, and her family didn't have time to listen to her pain or troubles. She became a teenage runaway, received a bump on the head, and found herself in a land she had never known.

Her family probably wouldn't approve of the friends that she picked up along the way either. Each of them had problems of their own. What they all had in common was the hope that they would find the thing that would make them whole. So they traveled together, each helping the other. In each other, they found a listening ear without judgment.

They faced a lot of trials along the way. Trials that made them grow stronger, together and individually. They overcame them one by one. What they found at the end of their journey was that they were never missing anything to begin with. They had all the things that they went out into the world seeking in the first place. Until they went through the journey and the hardships though, they didn't know what they were made of or the power within.

The girl is Dorothy; her story is the Wizard of Oz. Remember the Scarecrow, the Lion, and the Tinman? They each sought things that they already possessed.

Until we know Christ, and the power of the Holy Spirit, we will venture off trying to find the love and peace that he has already provided for us at the cross. The trials of life teach us what we are made of, and it is only when we look for and turn to the greatest wizard of all that we will know the truth about our identity! Christ died to cover our feet in those ruby red slippers—red with *his* blood, forgiving us and redeeming us every step of the journey.

Never regret the "Yellow Brick Road" as every brick has a purpose in it. Pray for those friends to journey with, that will love you where you are as you help one another along the way. Tell your stories to one another and sing songs along the way. Be prepared though. Life will throw apples, and there will be flying monkeys and fields of poppies to numb you! Stick together and just keep steppin'!

Know that there is a God that says there is a purpose to *every* thing under the heavens. Turn to Jesus, thank him for those ruby red slippers. Forgive others, forgive yourself, forgive God if necessary. Above all, keep walking down that road on the truth seeking journey until you discover that he is all that you need, and that he was with you all along.

"Because, because, because, because—of the wonderful things he does!"

Psalm 139:16: "Your eyes saw my unformed substance; in your book were written, every one of them, the days that were formed for me, when as yet there was none of them."

Chapter 91

Last year, I received a call to do two funerals, one on Monday, and one on Wednesday of the same week. I had never met either of the deceased. Went Sunday and met the family for the Monday funeral. Conducted Monday's funeral and set up the time Tuesday to meet with the other family before the Wednesday funeral. Got all that? Okay. The little lady I was burying Wednesday was a little eighty-nine-year-old Indian woman that loved to knit. I got to the funeral home Tuesday night and went in to see the family and view the body. They said the family wasn't there, so I went in to "meet" the woman I was memorializing.

You know how you have a certain idea in your head of what someone looks like? Welp, I did. And I was shocked. In the casket was a body with a flannel shirt, overalls, and a buzz haircut. There were pictures of semitrucks and even a toy one in the casket! I tried to understand if "she" lived an alternate lifestyle or *what* I was looking at and *how* that fit with the picture the family gave me on the phone. After a full minute, I began to look around and then saw the name of the person—and it was a dude! He was a sixty-year-old trucker! I was at the *wrong* funeral home looking at the *wrong* body!

Cleared up the confusion, walked across the street to the other funeral home (same owners, easy mistake people!), and found my eighty-nine-year-old Indian woman.

Chapter 92

Another dreary rainy day. Somehow I managed to get myself up and my children off to school, and, despite the heaviness of my soul, went to work. It had been one of those weeks in hospice. Some weeks held more death than others, and this week was one of them.

I pulled into the nursing home parking lot, preparing to make my visits. I hate umbrellas, so I dashed (okay, in my mind it was a dash—it was more like an epileptic on fire) through the downpour into the facility.

One of my visits was to a woman I will always remember. Every time that I visited, Mrs. Smith was dressed immaculately with matching jewelry and beauty shop hair.

She seemed out of place there among the other residents. There were no noticeable signs of the disease that was taking her life. We had wonderful conversations about the Lord, and she confessed her greatest fear to me.

She feared her mind would take her to a place that she would forget the love and goodness of God. We had many conversations about his faithfulness as we prayed for her peace and soundness of mind. I assured her that wherever her mind and that disease took her, God would be there too.

On this rainy day, however, I was once again the student as I entered the sunroom for a visit with Mrs. Smith. She sat there regally, now confined to a wheelchair.

We watched the rain come down in sheets as it had all week. The rain in my heart was threatening to drown me as I bobbed desperately in the sea of death that week.

I made a comment to Mrs. Smith that it would sure be nice to have a break from all the depressing rain. With the wisdom only garnered in years and years of living, she looked at me and said, "Somewhere a cow must need a drink."

As she said it to me, I saw it click for her as well. We shared a moment of healing and wholeness warmed by his presence and love.

"Somewhere a cow must need a drink."

Wow. In other words, God knew what he was doing, and it was bigger than my own limited view and perspective. We complain about the rain, when somewhere God is using it to give *life*.

Not just life to a cow on a hillside. The rain in my life watered my dry and barren soul. It took years, but finally green sprouts are coming through the soil.

I was surrounded by death in hospice, that God may teach me life and living. Thanks, Mrs. Smith. Every time we have an extended period of rain, I think of her and smile. God didn't just give a drink to a cow—he gave living water to two thirsty women that day.

Thirsty? Have a drink.

Chapter 93

Long, long ago, in a land far away, I owned a daycare center in Nevada, Jacob's Ladder. So many children and parents went through the doors in the course of those few years.

There are many "interesting" things that you deal with in childcare, just as in every field. One thing that is common in all businesses is maintenance and repair issues. My girls and I were all pretty handy to do whatever needed to be done. Occasionally, we had to have a little help.

Such was the case when one of the little toilets in the boy's bathroom began having problems flushing. Typically, we could see a toy and grab it with the handle thingy.

Such was not the case this time. We had to take the whole toilet up to find the offending bright red ball and Legos that were trapped.

After removing the toys, we had to put another wax seal on the toilet to secure it once again. Nothing hard, just tedious, especially when you are a bathroom short with fifty kids.

So why the big long story? Because I'm windy. But I also was reminded today of this story, and it made me reflect. There have been many things that I have tried to suppress or even hide. Things that

I don't want to have to deal with or think about because of the cost involved. Things I have tried to flush away.

Those things we shove down will back up our system and cause major plumbing issues until they are removed. And it's a stinky, messy process. If you get angry easily for no reason, you may have a red ball blocking your toilet. If you can't find peace, you may have some rogue Legos to recover and deal with.

The best way to maintain a healthy system is to walk in transparency, truth, and love.

We get shocked when sewage backs up in our life, yet it's the very stuff we refused to deal with a thousand times.

I had more than a bright red ball and some Legos blocking my path. However, I got that sucker cleaned out and now I refuse to brush things under the rug or flush things down the toilet—trust me, it all has a way of coming up anyway.

So speak and live your *truth*. The world's such a cleaner place when we do.

Chapter 94

I take her everywhere and have for years. Lucy is my road dog. She rarely leaves my side as I walk around performing my daily tasks. The other day was no exception. I took her to Muskogee with me, about a fifty-mile drive one way.

Lucy stays with her granny (Kathy Smith) or Aunt Tammi Benge Sawyer while I do my massages or running. After a full day, I picked Lucy up to head home. It was late and I was really tired. Lucy normally rides in my lap, but she jumped into the backseat to sleep. I guess she was exhausted too.

Well. Those that know me know that my mind tends to . . . wander. I had been driving about twenty minutes, with my radio blaring, singing off-key, when something flew between the seats, landing in the passenger seat beside me.

I let out a small scream and swerved the car for a second, certain I was about to be abducted and strangled by a furry, one foot tall angry midget or something.

Of course, it was the dog I had long since forgotten was even with me. My heart was pounding as I looked sheepishly around, glad for the darkness of the night surrounding me.

I kept on trucking as I was on a mission, headed home.

There have been people and things in my life that I blamed for all my fears. It was their fault that they showed up in my life out of nowhere, causing me such fright when they "jumped" at me.

The thing is I realized that I was the one that brought those fears along for the ride. They were my traveling companions, following my every footstep, like Lucy.

After I screamed and wrecked my life, I realized not only what was in my car, but that I had whistled to it and had it jump in the backseat!

Now, before I even set down at the wheel, I make sure my companions are love, joy, peace, patience, kindness, goodness, gentleness, faithfulness, and self-control. I invite them for the ride by giving control to the Holy Spirit. Then it is truly I that am along for the ride.

If you have fear, lies, and doubts in your life, know that you invite them. You have the power (through the Holy Spirit) to kick those things out of your car and life.

When I became accountable, I became powerful. God can't give us power if we won't be accountable and responsible with it.

We have places to go! Kick that junk out and make room for some new traveling buddies!

After all, "LIFE is a *highwayyyyy*, and I wanna drive it *alllll nightttt longgggg* . . ."

Chapter 95

Our church has been praying for people's hearts to be softened before our Saturday event that they may receive and hear his amazing love. We have thanked him for all the rain—what else to soften the soil of people's hearts with?

Well. I've been crying since Monday as he has overwhelmed me and broken up more hard soil in my heart—I had no idea there were still places of deceit that God is delivering me from.

Yesterday early a.m., I had a vision . . . part of it was seeing a symbol of one of my childhood sexual abusers, that I had "forgiven," and it was now a beautiful picture of God's love instead of what it was.

Hours later, I am on a friend's couch, talking to a guy I just met. He has been labeled something he is not, and as I convinced him that no matter what, he is not a label, he is forgiven, I "saw" his label before he told me. It was the same one "my abuser" wore.

As I sought to convince him to give his ashes to God, I felt as if I were talking to that man from so long ago that did that to me—that did that to *himself*, and it was so healing as I begged him to forgive himself because Jesus *has*.

As the guy began to talk, he mentioned his nickname. It was the exact same one as . . . *not* my abuser, but a broken man that made a broken choice in a moment of time, but was made whole and complete by a loving God for all time.

So thankful for the Master's tiller that breaks up the soil of our hearts, that we may find ever-new ways to glorify him as he heals us home.

If that's what it takes to please you, Jesus send the rain.

Chapter 96

I tried to scratch it off, just like I do every summer. I was surveying the seed tick attached just below my rib cage. As my vision has failed these last years, things are more and more difficult to see. Especially small things.

I tried to scrape the small offending bloodsucker off of me.

When I went to feel where it was, I couldn't feel . . . anything. When I couldn't feel anything, I realized that it was not something attached to me that I could free myself from.

Because it was a freckle.

A freckle! I remember that every summer, after I have gone through the seed tick routine at least once. It's not attached to me, it *is* me. This dark spot. This . . . thing. It doesn't look like the cream-colored skin around it. It's dark brown and shaped weird.

I can hate my freckle or love and embrace it. We all have our freckles, our dark spots, those things we are trying to rid ourselves of that are a part of the fabric of our being. Those things that look different from the smooth creamy places of my life . . . I have tried to pull them off, thinking them bloodsucking parasites, making me look hideous. Freckles from abuse, mine and others.

When I can understand that the one that knit me together is the one that put the freckles on me, or allowed (Job and Peter-Satan had to get permission to sift both) me to burn them into my own skin, I am *free*.

That means . . . he knows! He knows my freckles are there, and *they* are the very reason he sent his son to the cross. Not my creamy white skin. My freckles filled with child molestation and abuse. My freckles filled with murder and death and the decay of my mind. My freckles filled with my own addictions, abandonment, and ways I abused others.

Self-righteous pride and sarcasm filled my speech, until—until I could see my own freckles, instead of my neighbors.

For every freckle, every dark spot among the light, I give him all praise and glory and honor—for it is in the dark that I found the light.

Take all your freckles to God. He is the one that knit you freckle by freckle, valley by valley.

The freckles hold our faith. Got freckles? Good news, we all do! Better news? They are teeny tiny in the grandness of the grand design, yet they make such a contrast that it makes the grand . . . *grander*.

Thank him for all of your dark spots, and the light will overwhelm you!

Chapter 97

The desire began many years ago, I can't really say when.

Bar Church was something I have wanted to do for years. When I was lost and trying to find my way, one of my crazy ideas was staying in Florida and starting Bar Church.

Some time ago, Tammi Benge Sawyer introduced me to her friend that owned a bar. He knew me from a funeral that I had conducted. Craig W. Morgan and I hit off as I told him someday we needed to do Bar Church.

We found ourselves in New York far from Muskogee and any ideas and plans that we had.

While in New York, one of Tammi's friends, "Mary," fell or jumped from a balcony in Hawaii and was killed leaving two sons to deal with the pain and loss. Tammi clearly heard her friend say "I'm okay," and her grief became bearable.

Fast forward to now.

I kept feeling that I wanted to go to the bars and hand out flyers for our event "Liberty for *all*."

Tammi said that Craig Morgan was playing at the Eagles, and we had both been wanted to see and encourage him. We loaded up with our flyers with the intent of just hearing Craig play a song then leaving flyers on cars.

As we arrived, Tammi looked around at the handful of people scattered here and there. As we spoke, she said, "There is Mary's son playing pool."

Mary her friend that died in Hawaii.

We went over and Tammi hugged him and told him who she was. He was in his early twenties and was playing pool with another guy.

He was very polite, yet a little guarded. I asked his name, and when he said Nathan, the Bible story of David and Nathan began spilling from my lips as I encouraged him.

I told him and his buddy the story as they listened intently to the crazy woman in a bar telling Bible stories.

I concluded, "So yeah, Nathan was a stud! He jacked up David, a king."

I looked at Nathan's friend and asked his name. They looked at each other, then back at Tammi and I as he laughingly said, "David."

Wow!

Craig Morgan was there. Bar Church finally happened, but not at all like I envisioned it. It is seldom the way we see it as we see in part and prophesy in part.

What are the desires of your heart? Preaching in a bar has been a desire of mine for a long time, and God graciously fulfilled it as well as meeting the needs of another. That's the key. Meeting the needs of others. I have tried to do that all of my life without allowing God to meet mine (He did anyway, He's good like that).

You just never know who and what God has for you, just know that he is crazily romantic and loves to make is giggle!

I know Mary giggled as we reminded her son of her love and God's love in a dark tiny bar and had a church service.

Tammi, Craig, and I hugged and encouraged one another in our gifts, then IndianChick and I took off. We marveled at how Bar Church had finally come about, his way, in his perfection.

Who knew we would meet David and Nathan, too? We are all characters in a great story. Live one page at a time. Just be sure to actually *live* because he does!

I saw him in a bar.

Chapter 98

I looked out of the window at the new sign towering above the toddlers playing in the front yard. "Jacob's Ladder Christian Daycare" was displayed proudly among all the brothel signs, and across from the "Moon Light Bunny Ranch" sign in Carson City, Nevada.

Jacob's Ladder was a gift from God in a very dark time in my life. Through the course of several years, hundreds and hundreds of children came through the doors as well as adults that would become lifelong friends.

I named my center Jacob's Ladder based upon the bible story as well as a devotional book I read every year through grade school into middle school titled "Climbing Jacob's Ladder." My middle son is named Jacob for the same reason as "Climbing Jacob's Ladder" was instrumental in my childhood faith.

As an adult, I have taken that hardbound book with me all across this country as I have searched desperately for his peace and his purposes. I placed that book on the bookshelf in my new pastoral office at the beginning of this year, marveling at the journey that little book and I have been on.

Just as Jacob wrestled with the angel, I have wrestled all of these years until I saw Jesus for *myself*. Part of my journey was as a hospice chaplain. I have written a book filled with stories of that time, but one particular family impacted my life as no other.

Eulice Armstrong named me PreacherChick as I sat by his bed-side while he walked home. I conducted his funeral and gave his wife, Fannie, a book, "Cinderella." I told her that there really is a "happily ever after" and to hang on for it.

His family became my family.

Less than one year later, Fannie was killed in a car wreck and joined Eulice, together in a perfected relationship made holy by Christ and heaven.

That summer, I performed her daughter's wedding ceremony with a picture of Eulice and Fannie looking on.

Then—my life unraveled.

Fast forward a few years. Now I preach in a church every Sunday while Eulice's brother, Johnny Armstrong, does music and sings a song over my heart.

Johnny encouraged me as I made "Not Church" YouTube videos in New York and has championed my writing from the beginning.

He purchased airtime for me to preach the gospel over the airwaves and is helping me with the publication of my first book.

The Holy Spirit put together an event, "Liberty for ALL," and on flag day, we proclaimed *good* news and sang praises from the mountaintop. Children played as clowns tied balloons and folks ate free hot dogs prepared by Da'Sawyers.

I had a gift to give some of the people responsible for the event and for changing my life.

For Johnny Armstrong, I had a book. I was going to give him one that was over one hundred years old, but then I saw that book in my office, *Climbing Jacob's Ladder.*

What?

I have had that since I was little, and it got me through some dark days . . . what will a child's devotion mean to him? But I knew it was to be that book. It meant so much more to me, making the gift more precious.

I had just left the cemetery having gone by and "seen" Eulice and Fannie, amazed at the journey that began with us in 2009.

Saturday came, the event was amazing, and I gave Johnny the book.

Last night, he shared his story that I never knew. Just days after Eulice crossed over, Johnny's twin sister, Cheryl, called him sobbing.

She had a dream that Eulice knocked on her door. She was so happy to see him, but he was in a hurry. He walked through the house and outside. He picked up a ladder as Cheryl tried to get him to slow down or stay. He went out to the cemetery and put that ladder in his grave.

After Johnny heard the dream, he knew that Eulice had visited and then told Cheryl the story of Jacob's Ladder. He told her that brother was just fine that he had stuff to do that he was busy climbing Jacob's Ladder.

Five years later on a mountaintop, hoping to change a city, God changed us.

As I gave him my book, "Jacob's Ladder," Johnny had such perfect knowledge and peace that his brother was indeed present. Johnny Armstrong and his family have changed my life and have been a huge part of me climbing *out* of my grave.

Jacob's Ladder bridged the gap between heaven and earth, bringing the two together. We saw Jacob's Ladder Saturday as heaven came to earth and a relationship that began from death was now filled with life.

Some people are our ladder, an instrument that God operates through to bring us higher and closer to his kingdom.

Thanks Uncle Johnny for *being* Jacob's Ladder to me.

Chapter 99

His eyes had been unable to hold mine each time we have spoken since we first met one another a few weeks back. Today, parts of his story spilled from his lips, seemingly against his will, as I listened to his words but *felt* the pain behind them.

"I don't believe in God. Not the same one you do anyway, if there is one."

I would have argued with him years back before God broke me. But wisdom held my tongue as mercy coursed through my heart for him. See, I had already had one deep conversation with "Smitty." During that conversation, he revealed that many years back, his seven-year-old son died of cancer after a very long struggle.

Imagine. Imagine your child, vomiting over a toilet, as they threw up not only the few tablespoons of food you had to coax them to eat for hours, but the poisons pumped into his body to kill what was killing him.

Imagine no more birthday cake on their birthday, no more toothbrush in the toothbrush holder. No first crush or prom or children.

Smitty begged for his son's life, yet watched him take his last breath. In the dark forest of his pain, Smitty found himself homeless. Homeless most of his life, he said today.

He told me about living in a tent in the woods for years. When he would see someone, he would move deeper into the woods. Winter found him crawling under people's houses, seeking warm he could find beneath the floorboards.

As the people above him slept in their cozy, warm, beds, a cold hungry stranger huddled beneath them in the dark. He lay on the dirt, surrounded by the things that are all so much scarier in the dark. Snakes and spiders. He lay there alone.

The Smittys of this world are *all* around us. Real people broken and wounded, seeking warmth and shelter from those that profess to have it.

When we have seen Smitty, we have seen his bedraggled appearance and smelled his alcohol.

We have not welcomed him into our warmth, shared our soup and our shelter with him. We have seen him and smelled him and forced him under our feet. Under our floorboards is any and every person we have held in judgment personally, and as the church.

Jesus died for the Smittys of this world. He will heal and bind up the wounded and brokenhearted *his way.*

We judge people for the broken things they do, instead of taking them to or being the healer to them. They stay homeless and huddled in the cold homes of our hearts and wishing they were in our congregations, awaiting us to open up the door to them.

I say, wake UP! No more sleeping while Smitty is cold, hungry, and alone. Like soldiers, it is time to tend the wounded, give shelter to the homeless, feed the hungry, visit the prisoner.

When we love Smitty, his kingdom comes.

Who is Smitty? Me. That part of me that thinks I don't belong in the light, that I don't deserve fellowship, that makes me want to hide deep in the woods.

Thank God he rescued me! Now, it's time to go back and get all the Smitties of this world.

We *all* deserve to live together in the light with the roof of salvation above us, the walls of his mercy and grace surrounding us, the rock of Jesus Christ under our feet, all that we stand on that is noble and true.

It's time to rip up the floor boards of vain imaginations that has separated us, invading the dark underground with the light from above as we reach down and lift up those huddled in pain below.

It's time to go get Smitty.

Chapter 100

We've all seen them. And now, they actually have a *permit* to do what they do.

Unbelievable!

When I saw the blaze orange construction workers vest, I knew we had entered a new low as a society. The beggars on the streets of Muskogee are no longer few and far between. The city now requires them to buy a $35 peddler's license and wear a vest as they move from corner to corner.

One of these characters reminded me of John the Baptist the first time I saw him. John the Baptist looked like a wild man, wore fur, lived in the wilderness, and ate locusts. Not your average Jew, to say the least. This guy looked to be in his late fifties with a long scraggly beard and greasy unkempt hair. His clothes looked like the dirt was the only thing holding them together.

I have been preaching some about John, so I figured that is what turned my mind to him as well as I was preparing to baptize in the lake. As I came upon the beggar, I heard in my spirit, "I was hungry, and you fed me."

Well. I was in a hurry! I had a million little things to do before our "event," "Liberty for All" on Saturday. I was working for the Lord after all!

I figured it was just me remembering that particular scripture. So I rolled up to the stop sign as I smiled at the man. Just as I began to pull out, he held up his tiny sign:

Hungry
Broke

His blue eyes were piercing and startling all at the same time.

It made my stomach hurt and my heart sad as I heard once again, "I was hungry and you fed *me*" in my spirit. God protected me because I did a *U*-turn in that intersection at about twenty miles an hour.

I pulled into KFC, no idea what to feed the man. Then I decided to keep it simple and just order what I would order for me.

I got my order and parked my car. As I stomped through the uncut grass toward him, he surveyed me warily.

I crossed over the road, extending the bag and drink to him slowly, as you would approach a frightened puppy.

Let me say, that while I am sure it looked like a holy endeavor, the voices in my head were having a field day.

"This is crazy! He's probably gonna bludgeon me with the stop sign!"

"Just stay calm. Even though he looks like *every* bad guy ever on Scooby Doo."

"Run into traffic!"

I hushed the voices as I attempted to start a conversation. After he had spoken more than one word, I realized he has "special needs."

In a limited voice with obvious hearing as well as speech impairment, with broken syllables everywhere, he began to spill out a little of his heartbreaking reality.

"Peopttle day datt why don't you dett a dobb? I day have *you* ebberr tood on your feet for eight howerrr in da sun? People dwibe pat me, and day yell mean tings and throw tingzz at me. I judd tay 'hab a nice day."

My eyes filled with tears as I not only heard but felt his pain and the pain of Jesus at the harming of one of his little ones. All I could think of was John the Baptist. This man is preparing the way, showing love in the face of hate. I told him that God had spoken to me twice, and shared how special and loved he was by his creator, and what a stud he was for loving the unlovable.

As we talked, his eyes were darting around. I wondered at this until later a friend told me that they "work" for someone else.

Years and years ago, at some point . . . no judgment, but many put their "special needs" loved ones into cold facilities. Then our state closed down the facilities, turning many people into the streets as they had no independent living skills.

Now, we judge those people as they stand on our corners and beg, exploited just like a prostitute as we scream "go to work you bums!" at the weakest of the weak, exploited by the evil.

I submit that *we* are the ones with "special needs." I am reminded of the scripture, "Is it nothing to you, all you that pass by?"

I am praying for direction because I want to go all Rambo and shut this thing down going on in *our* backyard.

After my brief encounter with the kind man, I began to walk away. Knowing I would never forget him, I still wanted to know his name.

I turned back and said over my shoulder,

"Hey, what's your name, brother?"

With those piercing blue eyes, he looked through mine and into my soul as he said, "John."

Chapter 101

Most of our relationship could be summed up by a moment we shared back in 1977 while visiting our grandparents in California. I was seven years old, and my sister, Michele, was fourteen. I had just bought a tie-dye skate board at the flea market and really thought I was something!

I was practicing in my grandparent's driveway, when the skate-board slipped out from under me, rolling down the driveway. I shot after it, not thinking of anything but saving that precious combination of cheap plastic and wheels.

The next thing I remember, my sister has me jerked up by my shirt, yelling at me. I had run right into the path of an oncoming car, her screeching front tires coming within inches from my head as I bent down to retrieve my board. My sister snatched me back just in time.

The lady was very shaken up, and my sister almost beat me to death. I'm not so sure that the car wouldn't have been less painful and traumatic! After I quit shaking, I got back on my skateboard.

That has been the case, not only in my life, but in the lives of so many that have been impacted by my sister. She has served her community and her children's school all of her adult life. Hours and hours of counseling, sessions have taken place at her kitchen table as she feeds whoever shows up, whenever they show up.

I don't know how many people have been within inches of destruction before being pulled back by the kindness and acceptance of my sister, a truly beautiful soul that accepts people where they are and lovingly encourages them to get back on their skateboard, but to use a little more wisdom and caution the next time.

While I devoted many of my years to "ministry," my sister devoted hers to ministering. She always has been, and always will be, my lifesaver.

Bedsores and Butterflies is for anyone that has ever experienced pain or needed hope. Reader's that have reviewed the book say:

"Inspiring!!! A tender word for the grieving heart."

Lorena Dennis

"Smilen' Tears!!"

Tammi Sawyer

"I could read forever and never get enough. I get chills and tears every time I read!!!!"

Shannon Smallwood Vidacak

"Barbie has the rare gift and ability to present stories which pull at her reader's heart chords, whether or not they have experienced a similar situation. Her grasp on language, experience, spirituality, humanity, pain, love, evolvement and humor make for a gripping read with every story she tells."

Faith O'Connor

"In the darkness of life events, the author brings the love of God to light in each chapter."

Richard Merritt

About the Author

Madeline L. Engle said, "Stories make us more alive, more human, more courageous, more loving."

Barbie Smith has been a storyteller all of her life. She shares her stories in hopes that others will be inspired in their own story, and to tell their own stories. Her faith and humor have been her anchors throughout the trials in her life.

Barbie has three grown sons, Nicholas, Jacob, and Joshua. They are the pride of her life and articulate young men. She spends her life with her soul mate, Sean. She recently acquired a bonus son, Mitchell, whom she loves dearly despite his red hair. She is the Pastor of Liberty Community Church and the host of a weekly radio program. When she isn't preaching or teaching, she loves to spend time walking the lakeshore with Sean, painting on her deck, or laughing with her friends and family. She is currently working on her next book.

CPSIA information can be obtained at www.ICGtesting.com
Printed in the USA
LVOW07s2044030215

425545LV00003B/237/P